The Rolling Desk

A Story Of How Lasting Success Depends On A Purposeful and Well-Defined Company Culture

David J. Morris
CEO of Dillanos Coffee Roasters

Chris Heyer
President of Dillanos Coffee Roasters

PRESS 22 PUBLISHERS
1607 45TH STREET EAST, SUMNER, WA 98390

For more information contact:
PRESS 22 Publishers
800-234-5282

ISBN Hardcover: 978-1-939758-73-6
ISBN Paperback: 978-1-939758-90-3
ISBN eBook: 978-1-939758-74-3

CONTENTS

Dear Reader,

This book is an invitation to step into the story of a company called Callahan Coffee Roasters. It's a business fable, designed to spark ideas, conversations, and a renewed passion for putting the culture of a workplace first. Many companies get things backward: It's easy to forget that people make the profit. This story is about remembering that companies survive and thrive on their values, and that is when financial success *will* follow.

We know this because it worked for our company, Dillanos Coffee Roasters. The stories you'll read in these pages are all based on the true stories of Dillanos. A few years ago, David wanted to understand the business he was running from the inside out, and something told him that the only way to do that was to know its people. So he went to Ikea, bought a little rolling desk on wheels, and spent a week in each of the company's departments. This book is based on that experience.

The eleven Core Values we'll share with you in this book are the actual core values we live by at Dillanos—the values that define the running of our business. All of the anecdotes are real: Some tell of approaches we've used in the past, others detail approaches we continue to use every day, and a few show approaches we are in the process of implementing for the future.

Part of the process of writing this book has been about reviewing and improving Dillanos, and hopefully offering you some new ideas to take into your company.

All of the stories you'll read in this book represent strategies that work. We've seen them yield results in terms of the quality of our company culture—and, following almost automatically, the success of our business. So turn the page. Join Dillanos on a journey of change and growth.

—David J. Morris and Chris Heyer

Acknowledgments

We would like to thank first and foremost all of the wonderful past and present employees of Dillanos Coffee Roasters. Without them our special company, which inspired this book, would not exist.

Thank you to Teresa, Sara, and Michael.

Thank you David and Marni Heilbrunn from Coffee Fest. Thanks to Keith, Rand, Phil, Jeff, Mark, Melissa, and Lon for their valuable help and input. Thanks to Larry Green for his mentorship and Kathy McMahon for the motivation. Thank you to Chris Richter for the introduction to specialty coffee and Stephen and Sandy Peterson for the opportunity.

Thank you Chris Widener, Chris LoCurto, Marty Cox, and Andrea Waltz for your valuable testimonials.

Thank you to our beautiful mom whose lovely personality is always a shining light in every room.

A special thanks to David's stepdad and Chris's dad, Howard Heyer. What a great partner and person. He has taught us to be generous and hardworking and to never give up. Since 1992 his wisdom (and capital) has been infused in our company, making it a solid business that we can all be proud of. Thank you to David's dad Jeff Morris for his creativity and inventiveness.

Of course a big thank you goes out to our beautiful wives Celeste and Julie. Our children Dillon, Skylar, Hannah, Ava, and Rogue: Thank you for going on an entrepreneurs' ride.

Thanks to our brother Casey, who is such a great husband, father, and man to his family.

Thanks to all of our great vendors and loyal customers.

As with anything like this, we could literally list thousands of people that have helped or inspired us. So one last thank you to ALL of you. You know who you are.

"Not What We Ordered"

DOUG THOMPSON had been staring at the corner of his desk for more than twenty minutes. His eyes were fixed arbitrarily on a nick in the well-worn surface of the wood desk. He couldn't remember when he'd made that particular scratch; by this time the twenty-year-old desk was crosshatched with scars and dents like the paint job on a rusted-out junkyard car, kept only for spare parts.

Maybe he'd banged it one of the many times he'd moved offices as the company expanded and built new headquarters. Or maybe he'd accidentally chipped it back in the days when he used paper ledgers and piled the desk high with heavy books. Or maybe one of his grandsons had scratched it as he raced his Hot Wheels round and round the edge of the desk while Doug tried smilingly to work.

Doug was in trouble, and for the first time in his long career, he didn't feel like fighting it out. His head felt heavy and thick, and his heart literally ached. His company was in jeopardy. More importantly—*far* more importantly—all the people in his company were in jeopardy. He was responsible for their livelihoods, for the livelihoods of their families, and he felt like there was a good chance he would fail them.

Doug had founded Callahan Coffee Roasters two decades earlier. He'd taken a passion for good coffee and good customer service and thought, "What the heck? Why not see where this goes?" And so he'd created Callahan, a wholesale coffee roasting company, and started selling to independent coffee shops and cafés in Mandrake Falls, his small West Coast city. Twenty years later, Callahan had a customer base of over a thousand coffeehouses all across the United States.

As the company began to have some success, Doug set down on paper the eleven Core Values that formed the basis for his approach to business—and to life, really. He sought out workers who were willing to put the Core Values at the forefront, so much so that the Callahan staff recited all eleven of them at every Monday Morning Meeting.

Sure, Doug had an unflagging commitment to the business, and he loved coffee, but what mattered most to him was creating a home for his employees, a place where people challenged and supported each other. It was no small wonder that the company had won the Best Place to Work award in the region's business journal three years in a row. Callahan's mission statement:

HELP PEOPLE
MAKE FRIENDS
HAVE FUN

That was it.

And it had always worked. Until now.

Callahan had run into bitter times. About a month before, they'd lost more than 20 percent of their business when their largest customer was bought out by a multinational chain.

Just a few years ago, Doug would have brushed off such a setback with hardly a hiccup. The loss of that customer had nothing to do with the quality of Callahan's product or staff; it was just business. And he felt sure of the foundation he'd built beneath Callahan; he knew it could take the hit and come back strong. The problem was ... he didn't know if he was the man for the job anymore. He was nearing seventy, and his wife had been diagnosed with heart disease. Doug thought of Callahan as his family, but what he wanted most now was time at home, and what Callahan needed most was someone who could come in fully committed, with a clear head—and a clear schedule. Doug's gut told him it was time to let new talent, and new passion, step in.

What was gnawing at him, though, was that there was no one in the company ready to take on the job. It would have to be an outside hire.

Doug drummed his fingers on the rough surface of the desk. A résumé was laid out before him, several pages long. At the top of the first page, a simple embossed typeface called out a name: *Max Anderson.*

A turnaround guy. Almost serendipitously, Doug had met him at a conference only six months before. And a month ago, when the double whammy of losing 20 percent of his business and learning his wife's diagnosis had hit him in the same week, Max's name came instantly to mind.

Doug remembered a smiling, fair-haired man, still young for the relative renown he was starting to garner in the Pacific Northwest's business community. Max was soft-spoken and charmingly self-deprecating, yet at the same time, he managed to exude a relaxed confidence. When he walked into the room, a sense of ease followed him. He seemed to be saying, "Don't worry. I got this."

Doug had been glad to meet him, and the two had shared drinks after an evening seminar. He even remembered thinking at the time, "I wish there were some project or enterprise I could team up with this guy on." Something about Max made Doug think, "We see eye to eye." But of course, when they had met, things were going strong with Callahan; Doug's executive team was in place, and he didn't have a position to offer Max that would be appropriate.

But now Doug was in a very different position, staring down at Max's résumé and wondering if he should offer this near-stranger the reins of the company he had founded. Max was only in his early forties, but his résumé told the story of six different companies that he had brought back from the brink, all with profiles very similar to Callahan's. The trouble was, Doug recognized some of those companies. He knew managers at a few of them. And he knew what they looked like before Max ...and after Max.

As far as Doug could tell, Max Anderson's approach

was to streamline. He cut companies down to their bare bones. Sure, it made for efficient operations and enviable overhead. But was it the right approach for Callahan? It was a move that would make Doug cringe, after so many years of building the business around its people. First of all, he was hardly a clunky operator; he never created new positions, let alone departments, without double- and triple-checking to avoid redundancy.

Redundancy? The word left a sour taste in Doug's mouth. Callahan was like a hive, every role clearly defined, and every worker essential to his or her role. And just like a hive, Callahan's people depended on each other; their successes and failures were shared.

Doug knew full well that "company culture" can mean a lot of things; he'd seen the phrase overused and worn out by companies wanting to prove they had a heart. But at Callahan, "culture" went way beyond giving employees flextime or a table tennis kit in the lunch-room. When Doug said that his people mattered more than his bottom line—that, in fact, they *were* his bottom line—he meant it in a very real way.

Could he really call in an outsider known for slash-ing head count? Somebody who wouldn't understand the value of each employee on a day-to-day basis, way beyond a paragraph-long job description?

But then again ... Was that really who Max Anderson was? Doug had always trusted his instincts, and his instincts were telling him that there was something more to Max than the black-and-white story on his résumé. "All right," Doug thought. "Maybe I can persuade him to take a good long look at Callahan and the way we do things around here before he makes any decisions about how to reorganize the business. There's something about him that makes me think he's creative and flexible. Let's put him to the test."

Doug reached for the phone.

•••

"This is so embarrassing, Mr. Anderson—"

"Please, call me Max."

"Oh. Max. Of course. I mean, of course, this is definitely a first-name kind of place, I just wasn't sure ..." Rhonda trailed off. She was desperately trying to keep Max Anderson from seeing over her shoulder into the CEO's office behind her, but at the same time she was trying her best to put on a welcoming, warm face for her new boss and Callahan's new CEO.

It was an impossible juggling act. She gave up with a wan smile. "I'm so sorry, Max, but there's been a really embarrassing mix-up. I hate that this is what you're walking into on your first day."

She stepped aside and motioned toward the CEO's office.

Max walked through the doorway and into what looked like a disaster zone. All the ceiling tiles had been removed, and they were piled in a messy heap at one end of the room. On the far wall, the drywall had been torn away, and strips of paint hung around the hole, which showed studs and exposed wire. There were file cabinets against another wall, and a few chairs ... but no desk.

Max lifted an eyebrow with curiosity. "Remodeling?" he said.

"Yes," Rhonda replied weakly. "Well ... not exactly. I mean. We hadn't planned on it."

Now Max's curiosity was truly piqued. "Surprise remodeling?" he asked.

Rhonda was clearly uncomfortable. She lowered her voice. "It's absolutely my fault. See, Doug had this old desk. He's had it from the time he started the business; it's moved with him through three different offices. And it was a piece of junk!"

Max smiled warmly. Although they'd only been able to speak a few times before Max was rushed into his new position as CEO, he felt like he knew Doug, and he liked him—Doug was exactly the kind of laid-back boss who wouldn't think to update his desk for two decades.

"So at his retirement party last week," Rhonda continued, "he pulled me aside and told me he thought I should probably get that old desk replaced before you moved in. As a nice welcoming present to our new CEO. So I ordered a new one."

"That's very kind of you," Max said. "I'm sure it'll be great. But what about the ceiling?"

Rhonda sighed. "I thought as long as we were having facilities people coming in and moving out the desk, we might as well repaint the office; it hasn't had a new coat in a few years. And then I thought we should go ahead and replace that overhead light—Doug always used a desk lamp, so he didn't notice it was broken. But then when the electrician came in, he found a problem in the wiring, and it turns out they're going to have to redo the whole ceiling so they can put in a new series of lights. And then the new desk—the whole reason for this in the first place—didn't even come in on time, so it's just a complete fiasco!"

Rhonda looked down at her hands. "It's so awkward. We were so looking forward to meeting you, and we've got the Monday Morning Meeting starting in just a few minutes, and I'm not even sure where to tell you to put your coat ..." She trailed off again.

"Monday Morning Meeting?" Max said. "It's Thursday."

"Oh, that's just what we call it." Rhonda waved her hand as if this were the most normal thing in the world. "It used to be on Mondays, but then we changed it so the delivery drivers could come, and ... Anyway, it's not important. I'm just really sorry about your office."

Max passed a hand through his hair. "I don't know," he said. "Seems like it's kind of a chance for me to get a fresh start, right? New job, fresh office. It'll be fun."

"Oh," Rhonda said, visibly relieved. "Yeah, it could be fun."

Max rubbed his hands together. He'd been looking forward to getting started and meeting his new team. This wasn't exactly what he'd expected, but it was hardly a setback. "It's really no big deal," he said. "If you've got some time later, maybe you can help me pick out some new paint colors. Although I guess we will need to get some people in here to patch up the drywall once the electrician is done."

"I'm already on it," Rhonda said, brightening. She'd been Doug's executive assistant for six years, and she had get-up-and-go boiled down to a science. She flipped open a folder and pulled out a sheaf of paint swatches. "I'd be happy to look at these with you later on today. And the electrician should be here in an hour to get started on the lights. It shouldn't take more than a few days to get things in order. In the meantime ... I mean, if you don't mind, we'll set you up out here in Reception. It's a bit unorthodox, but it'll give you a real sense of the comings and goings of the place."

"You know, I've never done anything like that before, but I like the sound of it," Max said, pleased to find that the very first Callahan employee he'd met was already living up to Doug's rave reviews. "The only thing I really can't do without for the time being is a desk."

"Did somebody say 'desk'?" A voice called from down the hall.

Max and Rhonda turned to see a large cardboard box rolling toward them. A head peered out from behind it, and a moment later, Ted, the facilities manager, sidled the box up alongside them on a dolly.

"I think your new desk just got delivered, Mr. Anderson," he said cheerfully.

Max grinned and put out a hand. "Please. Call me Max," he said. "You must be Ted—I've heard a lot about you."

A strange expression passed over Ted's face. "Good things, I hope?" he said.

Max felt a small twinge in his chest. He'd seen that expression countless times before. It was inevitable: People knew who he was and what it meant when he took over a company. People got scared. He hated to see it; the last thing in the world that he wanted was to be the harbinger of bad news. But Max saw his role as the opposite. His job was to save livelihoods, not do away with them. He wanted to do his best to make sure the people at Callahan knew he was on their side. The unfortunate reality, though, was that the company was in trouble. His business school training and his decades of experience turning companies around had made him a firm believer that things often have to get a little worse before they get better. There would be some tough decisions ahead, and he couldn't guarantee the security of every position on staff.

Max wanted to do his best, however, to make sure everything was as painless as possible for the people he'd already come to like, through Doug's descriptions alone. He gave Ted a reassuring smile. "Only good things," he said.

"Good," Ted said, rallying. He clearly didn't want to be caught looking nervous. He pulled a pocketknife out of his belt and set about prying open the box. "Let's get you set up, then. Don't want to take any more time out of your busy first day."

The lid of the box fell away, and Ted pulled out a few Styrofoam packing pieces. He, Max, and Rhonda peered inside.

"Huh," Rhonda said. "That's definitely not what we ordered."

Inside the box was a small red desk, hardly bigger than a high school lecture hall desk. It had no drawers, no shelves, no frills. Max let his eyes pass over the surface of the odd little desk and down its thin, precarious legs.

"Well, that's strange," he said. "It's on wheels."

CHAPTER ONE

CORE VALUE #1
Always Possess Honesty, Integrity, and Loyalty

*Whoever is careless with the truth in small matters
cannot be trusted with important matters.*
—Albert Einstein

MAX FOLLOWED the receptionist down the hall, awkwardly
rolling his desk in front of him. It was hardly 11 a.m.,
and already he felt like his first day at Callahan couldn't
get any fuller.

After Ted had opened the box to reveal the odd little
desk, Rhonda could barely contain her embarrassment.
Things were not going well for her. She'd tried to get
everything right for Max's arrival, and just about everything that *could* go wrong *had* gone wrong.

Luckily, Max was the kind of guy who could sense
when things were veering off the track and steer them
gently back on course. Before Rhonda could start apolo-
gizing again, he made a few jokes about how the desk's

scrawny legs matched his own and got both her and Ted laughing.

"Besides, it's got wheels!" Max said. "It'll be way easier to get it out to the reception area like this. We won't even have to ask Ted to use his dolly."

Rhonda promised to put in a call to the office furniture supplier as soon as the Monday Morning Meeting was over to find out how the mix-up had happened and when the real executive desk could be delivered. And they all agreed to just take a break from the whole office-remodeling fiasco, leave the desk in the hall, and head to the meeting.

Little did Max know what awaited him. The last time he and Doug spoke, the man had told him with a chuckle, "You'll understand what kind of a place Callahan is once you've been to a Monday Morning Meeting. I won't even tell you what to expect—you've got to experience it for yourself."

It turned out Doug was right. Max had assumed Doug was chuckling because the meeting was one of those boring corporate affairs, where each manager droned on for their allotted ten minutes, and conversations went around in circles, and nothing of importance got accomplished. So he'd prepared some very brief remarks to introduce himself to the staff. Nothing fancy—his only goal was to keep things short, let everyone know that he was on their side, and adjourn so people could get back to work.

Instead, the Monday Morning Meeting proceeded on its own, and Max quickly forgot that he even had a checklist of remarks in his pocket. As they headed toward the meeting room, Rhonda said with a smile, "Doug usually ran these, but don't worry, I'll take the lead on this one until you get the hang of it." And Max was left to get swept up by ... what was admittedly the most fun "meeting" of his life.

When he walked into the room, the entire Callahan staff erupted in cheers. Rhonda grabbed a remote control for the sound system and pressed a button, and the theme song from *Rocky* started blaring through the speakers.

"Ladies and gentleman, announcing ... the new Callahan Coffee Roasters C ... E ... Ohhhhhhh!" Rhonda shouted. Everyone started laughing, and Max was so surprised that he had to laugh, too.

"And now," Rhonda said, "the Callahan Wheel of Questions!" She gestured toward a wheel divided into colored sections, à la *Wheel of Fortune*. "Every new employee spins it—and every new employee answers the question they get."

Max had to oblige. He spun the wheel. It hummed around and then slowed to a stop. The arrow pointed to ... *What is your hidden talent?*

An expectant hush fell over the room.

"Uh ..." Max said. "Oh, I don't know. I mean, I'm pretty good at running a business."

"Boo!" someone in the back of the room shouted jokingly.

"Cop-out!" called someone else.

"They're right," Rhonda said. "It says, '*Hidden* talent.' Come on—think of something good."

Max sighed. "Okay, okay. There is something. I, uh ... I used to be in the juggling club in middle school."

The employees laughed and a few cheered. "Show us," said a young guy in a green T-shirt.

"Nah, it's not that great," Max said, embarrassed.

"Oh, come on!" Rhonda said. And pretty soon the whole room was chanting, "Show us, show us, show us!"

"All right, all right!" Max said. "Um ... okay, see those sample bags of coffee by the coffee machine? Somebody toss me three of them. One at a time."

A woman with bobbed brown hair was standing by

the coffee machine. She picked up a bag and tossed it to Max. He caught it, and immediately threw it in the air above his head—just in time to catch the second bag the woman tossed. Pretty soon, he had all three bags circling in the air. The employees cheered and clapped.

"Wait, wait, wait!" Max shouted, getting caught up in the excitement. "Toss me one more bag!"

She did. And without missing a beat, still keeping the other three bags in the air, Max caught it and tossed it up. He was juggling all four bags at once.

"Now—anyone got a butcher knife? Or a flaming torch?" he joked.

The "meeting" continued in the same vein. There were no reports. No handouts with figures and tables. Instead, the staff split up into teams, with employees from all the departments mixed up together, and played a couple ridiculous games Max had never heard of, even from his two elementary-school-aged kids. Most of the time, he couldn't stop laughing. The rest of the time, he was working on overdrive, trying to take in all the new names and faces. Every single employee was there, from the upper-level managers to the sales reps.

When it was all over, Max said, "I can't wait until next Thursday!"

"Ah," said Rhonda. "Our Monday Morning Meetings are only once a month. But don't worry—there's lots more fun in store for you."

So now, with all that excitement behind him, Max was in the rather undignified position of rolling his new, wheeled "executive desk" down the hall to his new "office"—the reception area. Luckily, the desk was a light little contraption, and he had to admit it cornered well. He smiled to himself. This would make a good story for his kids when he got home.

Finally, the hallway opened into a large, sunny room with a wall of windows at one end facing a long, gleaming reception desk. Angie, Callahan's receptionist, stood in the center of the room, smiling proudly. She was a bright-faced woman in her mid-thirties, with blonde hair pulled into a thick, curly twist, and she wore small, light-rimmed glasses.

"Here it is!" she announced. "Your temporary office!"

Max had of course already seen the reception area and met Angie several times as he was going through preliminary meetings with Doug and the Callahan board before he'd been officially hired as CEO. But he still had to admit, the room made a welcoming impression. There was a corner with a cozy couch and a few chairs, and several varieties of fresh-brewed coffee were arrayed on a low table. It was more than just the room you walk through before you get to the real business; it had a warm feeling. Max added the aroma of coffee and the feel of sunlight streaming through the windows to his mental list of things that felt right to him about Callahan.

He rolled the desk up to one of the chairs by the window.

"What do you think?" he asked. "Will I be out of the way if I set up shop over here?"

"I think it looks very official," Angie said with a wry smile.

As she made her way to her own chair behind the long reception desk, Max noticed a name plaque that read simply, "Angie." That was all, not even a last name.

Max decided he liked that. Anyone coming into the office would know it was fine to call her just by her first name—and even her nickname. Not Angela, just Angie. Max made a mental note to himself about that approach. He'd always hated his name plaques that read, "Maxwell Anderson." No one ever called him Maxwell anyway, so what was the point?

Max sat down and was just starting to open his laptop to review the projected budget Doug had sent him, when something crossed his mind.

"Angie, are you busy?" he asked. "Can I ask you a question?"

"Sure, no problem," she said, looking up from her computer.

"That sort of ..."—he searched for the right word—"*recital* you all did at the end of the meeting. Is that something you do every month? Or was that for my benefit?"

"You mean the eleven Core Values?" Angie asked.

That was exactly what Max meant. At the end of the Monday Morning Meeting, the employees had recited in unison the eleven Core Values.

Max was somewhat familiar with the list of values. Doug had given him a copy of them and told him very sincerely that these were the keys to the culture that Callahan lived by. So Max had read them with some interest, and thought that they seemed pretty useful and wise—if a bit unlike the value lists he'd seen at other businesses. And then he had put the document in his briefcase and more or less forgotten about it. To him, a company's mission and values were things you familiarized yourself with so that you could introduce the company to potential customers in a sort of flashy, elevator-speech kind of way; what really told a company's story were the books.

"When we say we live by the eleven Core Values," Angie said, interrupting Max's thoughts, "we really mean it. It's not just a cute poster on the wall. I can't tell you how many times they've been useful to me."

"Really?" Max asked. "How do you mean?"

"Well, when I've got a tough decision to make. I could do something this way or that way, and I'm not sure what's best for Callahan or the customer or the staff. If I just ask myself, 'What would line up with our values', the answer usually pops right out at me, clear as day."

Max nodded noncommittally. That sounded nice, but he wasn't sure he was convinced. He could imagine that following the guidelines in the Core Values gave Angie a pretty good standard of behavior as Callahan's receptionist, but he doubted they would apply to problems at the executive level. The values were pretty simple—and some of them didn't seem to have much to do with dollars and cents.

Just then, Max's thoughts were interrupted again as a tall, dark-haired man came in through the front door, carrying what looked like a heavy cardboard box.

"Hassan!" Angie cried, jumping up from her chair. She hurried around the desk and reached out her arms to help with the box, but Hassan shook his head.

"No, no, no, Ms. Angie, absolutely not!" he said. "It's not that heavy. See? It's like a toy—I can toss it in the air!" He made as if to toss the box ... but clearly it *was* too heavy, so instead he settled for smiling ruefully.

Angie laughed. "Don't drop my labels just because you're in a joking mood," she scolded. "You can set them down over here, and I'll have Ted bring them to Packaging."

Hassan set the box down in the corner.

"Oh, Hassan, there's someone I'd like you to meet," Angie said. She motioned to Max. "This is our new CEO, Mr. Max Anderson."

"Glad to meet you, Hassan," Max said, standing up and extending a hand.

"Pleased to meet you, too, sir," Hassan said. He glanced curiously at the little rolling desk, but seemed too polite to press any questions. "I'm with Danby Label Company. We do the labels for your coffee packaging."

"Oh, fantastic," Max said. "Keep up the good work. I look forward to introducing myself to our account rep soon."

Hassan nodded. "She'll be glad to know Callahan's in good hands," he said. Then he turned to Angie. "Kids all right?" he asked. "Jesse just turned six, right?"

"He did! Thanks for remembering," Angie said, beaming. "You'd never believe how tall he is."

Hassan grinned. "He's gonna be a starter, that kid." Then he turned toward the door. "All right, folks, I better head out to the next delivery. Have a good one!" And with that, he had disappeared again.

"Is he an old friend?" Max asked Angie.

"Hassan? Sure, I guess you could say that. I've been with Callahan ten years, and he's been with Danby something like fifteen, so he's been bringing their deliveries ever since I've been here. Our kids are about the same age, so we've gotten to know each other over the years."

"Callahan's been using Danby labels for ten years?" Max asked.

"I'm pretty sure it's more than that," Angie said. "If I had to guess, I'd say they've been with us from the start. Doug liked to work with vendors that share his take on company culture—if they were as committed to honesty, integrity, and loyalty as he was, then he'd try to build a lasting relationship with them. To him, relationships with vendors were just as important as relationships with customers."

"Didn't that sometimes lock him in with a vendor that might not have the best price?" Max wondered.

"Not really," Angie said with a shrug. "He saw it as a two-way street. A partnership. We give them loyal business, so they work with us to keep that business by treating us well. Same as we do with our customers."

"I like the sound of that," Max agreed. "If we want our good work to be rewarded, we should reward the good work others are doing for us."

"Exactly!" Angie said. "It might not be the reality with every single vendor. Of course, sometimes we've got to work with a national company that can't be as flexible or give us as much attention. But it's something to aim for. And, you know what, that goes right back to what I was saying about the Core Values. Our very first one—and it's number one for a reason, it's the most important—is ...

Always Possess Honesty, Integrity, and Loyalty.

And to me, that's not just a guideline for how we treat each other, it's how we represent Callahan to the rest of the world, too. It extends to our customers and vendors."

Just then, the door opened, and another delivery-man entered. He was carrying an enormous gift basket wrapped in plastic wrap and tied with a green bow. Max could see boxes of chocolate, cookies, fruit, candy, and other treats poking out of it at every angle.

"Got a delivery for ..."—the deliveryman checked the card attached to the bow—"Randy? That's all it says. Just Randy."

"Randall Morgan," Angie said. "Our CFO. I'll get it to him." She took the basket from the deliveryman, who gave her a warm nod, and headed out once again.

Max had given up on looking at anything on his computer screen—this was too intriguing. Why was the CFO getting a huge gift basket?

Angie seemed to have read his mind. "I know exactly who this is from," she said, taping the thank you card attached to the basket.

"Who?" Max asked.

"Oh, you'll love this story," Angie started. Then suddenly she caught herself, and her expression turned slightly worried. "At least ... I hope you will. See—we made a mistake. In the Finance Department. I'd say a pretty big one. We've got this major customer with a chain of coffeehouses all the way down the coast of California. And somehow—it was just a data-entry error—but somehow we overbilled them. Just a few cents per pound, but we didn't catch the mistake for nine months, and they're a *big* chain. So by the time we finally realized it, we'd over-billed them by about $10,000."

Max sucked in his breath. That was no small clerical error. Then again, a big chain might never notice a figure like that. It was doubtful they had anyone double-checking their invoices.

"So, as soon as we caught it," Angie said, "Randall called them up himself. He didn't want anyone else to take the fall; it was an honest mistake. It truly could have happened to anybody with all the numbers they're crunching. And the important thing is the employee who was responsible caught it, and told him about it right away. So he was able to call the customer and cut them a check for what we owed them." She smiled and motioned to the gift basket. "This is from them."

Max leaned back in his chair, beaming. "You know, I'm really starting to be impressed with the way you guys do things. It's that same Core Value—every single person in that story was completely honest and showed personal integrity. The responsibility was shared, and they made it right in the end."

Angie grinned. "I've been reading C.S. Lewis to my son, and you know what Lewis writes? 'Integrity is doing the right thing, even when no one is watching.'

I felt pretty proud to be a Callahan employee when I heard that story. Then again, I always have. That's why I've been here ten years. I've had a few offers from other companies to move up to something they would call a little 'higher-level' than Reception ... but I'd rather stay put. Do you know that Doug was present at every single one of my interviews? I had three, and he was there from the beginning. He said the receptionist is the face of the company. He really made me feel like this job is important. And I've felt that way for the whole ten years I've been here. Callahan has always made me feel valued."

Max smiled. "Good," he said. "I hope I can continue the trend."

· · ·

CORE VALUE #1

Always possess honesty, integrity, and loyalty.

We expect everyone to be completely honest at all times and consistently display personal integrity and loyalty. This attitude extends to our interactions not only with each other, but with our customers and vendors as well.

CHAPTER TWO

CORE VALUE #2
Give Our Customers More Than They Expect

A customer is the most important visitor on our premises. He is not dependent on us. We are dependent on him. He is not an interruption in our work. He is the purpose of it. He is not an outsider in our business. He is part of it. We are not doing him a favor by serving him. He is doing us a favor by giving us an opportunity to do so.
—Mahatma Gandhi

WHEN MAX arrived at Callahan the next morning, Rhonda met him at the door with a grim look.

"Your office isn't ready," she said. "The electrician says he needs a few more days."

Max had to admit it was a setback. As interesting and informative as the reception area was, he hadn't been able to get much done with all the comings and goings and new people to meet.

"Hmm," he said. "Okay—well, let's make lemonade out of these lemons. Or coffee out of these coffee beans."

He'd been planning to take a trip to the warehouse to talk to the managers there and take a look at how production worked—the coffee industry wasn't exactly old hat for him. Maybe he could roll his goofy desk along with him and make it a bit easier to take notes. So off he went. He decided arbitrarily to start with the Delivery Department—it was the closest open door as he approached the long warehouse building, and the little desk wasn't exactly easy to wheel along the concrete sidewalk.

He had barely made his way through the doorway when a big man with salt-and-pepper hair and a paunchy belly came striding across the floor toward him, skirting rolling carts and stacked boxes on his way.

He extended a huge, meaty hand and gave Max a broad grin. "The Juggling CEO!" he boomed. "To what does the Delivery Department owe the pleasure?"

Max accepted the hearty handshake and returned the grin. "I'm just getting to know the place and thought I'd stop in ... with my desk."

The man gave a loud, generous laugh. "I heard about your little mix-up," he said. "It's like back-to-school all over again."

Max nodded ruefully. "Sure does make me more mobile. It's Marty, right? Marty Bronson?"

"That's right! Good memory. Delivery Department Manager, at your service. But please just call me Marty," he said, clapping a familiar hand across Max's shoulders. "Would you like to join us for the day? It seems like you're hard up for an office. It can get a little noisy around here, but we're not hurting for space!"

"Well, sure," Max said. "I wanted to start getting a sense of how things run, so I might as well."

He followed with the little desk as Marty led him into a broad open space in the center of the concrete-floored room. On one side were huge rolling racks stocked with bags of coffee, and on the other side were large pallets, which men were loading with coffee and rolling out toward the open trailers of trucks backed into loading docks. Between the racks and the pallets, a man was checking the accuracy of each shipment as it passed from one side of the room to the other.

As they came up beside him, Marty introduced the man. "This is Todd," he said. "Checks all our shipments to make sure the right package is going to the right place. Our goal last month was 99.5 percent accuracy. Know what we got? 99.8 percent. Out of thousands of orders."

"Well, I'm pleased to meet such a superb employee," Max said, shaking Todd's hand.

"Hey, Marty!" Just then, someone called from across the room. It was a delivery driver, rushing up to Marty with a clipboard. He was dressed in the black and red uniform the delivery drivers wore. He held out his clipboard so Marty could see it. "I just wanted to remind you that my wife has her prenatal appointment late this afternoon, so I cut my route short by one stop so I can join her. It'll be our first time seeing the ultrasound."

Marty gave the man the same powerful handshake he'd given Max. "Of course I remember! Good luck to you. Phil's covering that last delivery, right? Should work out just fine."

Max couldn't help seeing the clipboard over Marty's shoulder. As the deliveryman was walking away, he said, "That was a pretty short list of stops. You don't think he could finish it all?"

"Not the way we do things," Marty said, clearly pleased with himself. "See, other companies might let their guys just pull their boxes out of the truck and drop them on the sidewalk by the coffeehouse's back door and drive off. The baristas are swamped, though. They've got a line ten deep of sleepy people who want their morning wake-up drink, and they don't have time for that kind of treatment. So our drivers carry the boxes in, stock the coffee bags neatly on the shelf, and then—just for kicks—pull out the full garbage bags, tie 'em up, and take them out to the dumpster for the baristas. How do ya like that for service?"

Max blinked at him, uncomprehending.

"It's Core Value number two!" Marty exclaimed, like that cleared everything up. "Here at Callahan, we ...

Give Our Customers More Than They Expect.

Those coffeehouses—they're our bosses. So why not go the extra mile for them?"

"But it must add so much time to the drivers' schedules," Max said, a little skeptical.

"It adds a little," Marty agreed, "but that little bit goes a long way with our customers." He paused, and smiled at Max with a twinkle in his eye. "You probably won't believe me when I tell you this—but I'm a couple decades older than you are. I was a kid in the '50s. You know, when the woolly mammoth still walked the earth. One of my favorite things was when my dad needed to stop for gas on the way home. We'd go to the filling station, and it was always full service. But the guy wouldn't just pump your gas, take his tip, and send you on your way. He wiped down the windows. Popped the hood and checked the oil. Topped off the tires if they needed it. And if I was lucky, if it was this one guy I really liked ... he'd reach in his pocket and pull out a piece of toffee for me. *That* was service. When did people forget how important that is?"

"I take your point," said Max. "I guess I just worry about efficiency. I mean, how much is really gained in terms of business versus all that time lost?"

"Lost? I wouldn't call it lost. I'd call it *invested*. First of all, think about those gas station attendants back in the '50s ... they didn't think of themselves as just gas pumpers; they were oil and tire checkers and general *service people*. They thought of the whole package as their job, not some extra nuisance they had to get through, and so they got really good at the whole package. They were like one-man pit crews. My delivery drivers are the same way—they think of the whole service as their job, and they get efficient at every part of it, not just the driving. And the small amount of time it does add, well, you'd be astonished how much of a difference it makes. You put in little gestures, it shows the customer you actually care.

It lets them know that we're in this to support their business; we're going to have their back."

"Tell me what you mean," Max said, intrigued.

"Okay ..." Marty was thoughtful for a moment. "Oh, here's a great example!" he said. "This was a long time ago—just a few years after Doug first founded Callahan. I remember this because I was there; I've been with Callahan from the beginning. We had a disaster. I mean, a disaster. We'd started expanding so our local drivers weren't enough anymore. We had some customers down in California, a few in some of the Western states. So we were using ShipExpress to get the product to those coffeehouses. But wouldn't you believe it: Their workers all went on strike. We couldn't use their competitor because they were completely overwhelmed by all the business ShipExpress already lost. We couldn't ship anything out."

Max nodded, remembering what Angie had said the day before. Sometimes you can't avoid having a somewhat impersonal relationship with a large vendor—and there are risks involved.

But Marty was already continuing. "There was this chain of coffeehouses down in L.A.—five coffeehouses— and they were scheduled to get a shipment in just a few days, and we couldn't figure out how to get it to them. It was going to be really bad for them. I mean, they would have zero coffee—they'd have to close up for the week. Who knows how that would have affected them? It could have been the end of their business.

"So you know what Doug did? He came to me and said, 'Load up a truck.' I did. And he got behind the wheel himself. Drove all the way to L.A.—something like twelve hundred miles—and delivered that coffee himself. And stocked their shelves and took out their trash, too."

Marty paused. Max sighed. He was just about to interject another question about efficiency and what kind of return Doug could possibly have gotten on that kind of investment of time. But then Marty jumped in, clearly pleased with his punch line. "Over the last ten years, that chain of five stores grew to a chain with over *one hundred* locations. And they will never buy a single coffee bean from anyone but Callahan."

Max leaned against the rolling desk thoughtfully. Marty had definitely made a good point with that one. Callahan's coffee was good; there was no doubt about it. But that might not always be all it took to seal in customer loyalty. Maybe that extra feeling of "We've got your back" really mattered a great deal.

"Marty, we were right!" A driver came rushing up. He was a short, stocky guy with a name badge on his uniform that read, "Carl."

"We were right!" he said again. "There was theft going on at Cuppa Joe. Probably the baristas."

"Oh yeah?" Marty said. "I gotta say, I'm not surprised. Something just wasn't adding up."

Max remembered Carl from the Monday Morning Meeting. "Hey there, Carl," he said. "What's this about theft?"

"Oh, hello, Max," Carl said, a little flushed, noticing Max for the first time. "Well, see, I heard somebody in Finance the other day say they were worried that Cuppa Joe was going to shut down. They were selling a lot less coffee than normal. And I thought, 'That's weird, because they keep ordering the same amount.' I deliver to them every week, and their orders hadn't changed a bit. So I'm thinking, 'Why would they keep ordering all that coffee if they're not selling it?'

"So I just kind of mentioned it to the morning manager as I was dropping off the order. Like, 'Is everything okay?' And he had *no idea*. He'd been doing their orders based on inventory; I guess he hadn't had a chance to get together with the manager who'd been keeping track of sales. So he looked things over while I was still there—and it looks like we were right. They've got some kind of internal theft problem. Probably the baristas pocketing the money for the coffee without ringing it up."

Once again, Marty put out his massive hand and shook Carl's with energy. "Nice work, sir."

And then he turned to Max with an amused little flash in his eye. "There it is again."

Max headed him off at the pass. "I know exactly what you're going to say," he said. "And you don't need to. I'm convinced. Surprise the customer. Give them more than they expect. It's obvious it's only going to help us both in the long run."

● ● ●

CORE VALUE #2

Give our customers more than they expect.

We will constantly go the extra mile for our customers. We remember that they ultimately sign our paycheck. We will strive to create value for our loyal clients because they are truly our bosses. "Exceed expectations" will be our mantra.

CHAPTER THREE

CORE VALUE #3
Be Creative and Resourceful

Creativity is a natural extension of our enthusiasm.
—Earl Nightingale

MAX CAME in on Monday morning with a plan. He was having a great time rolling his desk around Callahan, meeting and talking with its unique staff, but he was also beginning to feel a little guilty. He was starting to get the sense that Callahan was moving ahead on its own momentum, whether or not he contributed—but that didn't mean the company didn't have that 20 percent loss of revenue to contend with. He needed to sit down, get serious, and crunch some numbers. He needed to do the job he'd been brought in to do.

So, office or no office, he was going to get started. He decided he would set himself up in the Sales Department.

It had an open floor space where the sales representatives' desks were, and he'd noticed it was usually pretty quiet there because, at any given time, most of the reps were out selling. He'd already sent an email over the weekend to the director of sales and marketing, Jasmine Hillard, to clear it with her, and by 8 a.m. on Monday, he was sitting at his rolling desk in a quiet corner of the Sales Department, a steaming mug of Callahan's signature roast coffee beside him, and six different spreadsheets open on his laptop.

The trouble was ... something kept catching his eye.

Displayed on a small table against the wall near him was a big children's book. The title was splashed in yellow font across the cover: *Goldilocks and the Three Bears*. It was a silly distraction, but Max couldn't help being curious. What would a children's book be doing in the Sales Department of a coffee company?

He got up from his desk and went over to the book. It was over sized and bound in hardcover. Just as Max was about to open it up, Jasmine passed by on the way to her office. She stopped when she saw Max looking at the book.

"Oh, you found our sales work of art!" she said. She was a petite woman with a round face and dimpled cheeks that gave the impression that she was always smiling—which wasn't far from the truth. "We're very pleased with how it turned out."

"What?" Max said. "What do you mean?"

Jasmine laughed. "It's a little thing we came up with to show a potential customer our knack for creativity."

Max cocked his head, not getting it.

Jasmine was clearly amused by Max's confusion. "You know the story of *Goldilocks*, right? The fairy tale?"

"Of course," said Max. "My daughter loves it. Little Goldilocks gets lost in the woods; she finds the bears' cabin while they're out. She tries out everything in the house—the chairs, the porridge, the beds. Sometimes they're too big, too small, too hot, too cold, but there's always one that's just right."

"Exactly. Well, we've got this customer we just put together a proposal for. I sent you the profile, remember? Waterbury Coffeehouses, that chain of cafés on the East Coast?"

"Yeah, of course I remember," Max said. "They could be a huge account for us—in fact, I was looking it over, and I think it could be enough to get us back to last year's revenue numbers."

"Right!" Jasmine said. "We've been working really

hard on it. Their CEO and CFO came here for a tour a little over a week ago. I wish you had been here to talk to them, but it was just before you started."

"That makes two of us," Max said, regretfully. He would have loved the chance to make an impression on a customer that could make or break Callahan.

"It went really well, though," Jasmine said. "And this tiny thing that came up in our conversation gave us this idea. These guys were very corporate, suit-and-tie types, so we really tried to draw them out and have a good time with them—show them what Callahan's all about. I don't think you've had a chance to take our 'official tour' yet, but it can be a ton of fun. Usually people get here and tell me, 'Okay, I've got about an hour for this,' and they end up staying all afternoon because they're having such a good time. That's what happened with these guys."

Max was definitely pleased to hear that.

"Toward the end," Jasmine continued, "I was telling them why I thought Callahan would be the perfect fit for them. I told them, because of their size, most of our competitors just wouldn't be the right match. Like Wild Aspen Roasters—Waterbury would be a comparatively small account for them and wouldn't get a lot of attention; Wild Aspen is much too big. And some of these boutique roasters, they don't have the resources to really make Waterbury's brand shine; they're just too small. 'But,' I told them, 'Callahan is perfect for you. We're the exact right size.' And this very corporate CEO says, 'You're just right, like in *Goldilocks*.' "

Max smiled. He was starting to see where this was going.

"So I kind of took a mental note of that," Jasmine said. "It seemed like a great hook. Once they'd left, I had the Design Department scan a *Goldilocks* book, and look what we did." She opened the book up to the center page, which folded out. It showed a picture of Goldilocks tasting the porridge. On the bowl that was "too hot" was Wild Aspen's logo. On the "too cold" bowl was the logo of a boutique roaster, a small one Max didn't even recognize. And on the "just right" bowl—which Goldilocks was happily enjoying—was Callahan's logo. The Design Department had so seamlessly integrated the logos that it looked like the book had been illustrated that way.

"Hey, what's this?" Max asked, pointing to a little pin on the lapel of Goldilocks's red coat.

"That's Waterbury's logo!" Jasmine said.

"Wow," Max said, chuckling. "Really neat. Really creative."

"I sent a copy of the book to the CEO and the CFO. And I wrote a note saying, 'Looking forward to working with you. I know we'll be "just right" for Waterbury.' I've already had several follow-up conversations with them, and they can't stop talking about it. They thought it was a nice touch."

"That's great," Max said. "I mean, it's good to do something memorable. But do you really think it'll make a difference? In terms of their decision?"

"I think it's more than a gesture," Jasmine answered. "If we were creative enough to think of something like that, it gives them an idea of how we'll work with them in the future."

Max couldn't help feeling a little excited—Jasmine really seemed like she was on to something. "Great work," he said. "I'm planning to call the CEO myself. I'm sure you know what a big deal this could be."

"Absolutely," Jasmine said. "We're throwing all our resources behind it. Do you remember Core Value number three? At Callahan, we do everything we can to ...

Be Creative and Resourceful.

Especially in a department like Sales, it's something we see pay off in a very real way, all the time."

"Give me a 'for instance,' " Max said—not to challenge her, but because he was genuinely curious to know.

"Sure," Jasmine said. "I'm sure you know that trade shows are a huge way for us to get deals. Over the course of a weekend trade show, my reps might get hundreds of leads each. At other companies, reps take weeks to go through all those leads, and they'll send each one a form email saying, 'Great to meet you, blah blah,' and just change the name at the top of the message. That's it.

"My reps go straight back to their hotel rooms at the end of each day of the trade show, and the first thing they do is email every single lead a personalized message. And they make sure it's very specific and warm, and it connects back to the conversation they had with that person.

"The first thing they ask each prospective customer they meet is 'What's the most important thing about coffee to you?' So they've got something right there to continue the conversation with. They might write in their email, 'Here's how Callahan can support you with the goal you mentioned,' or 'Here's how Callahan can address this particular challenge you have.' So, by the end of the evening, that coffeehouse owner is going to be astonished to *already* have an email in his or her inbox from Callahan."

"Nice," Max said.

"But that's not it!" Jasmine continued. "The reps send me all the contacts they gathered, and I also send them an email saying how much we enjoyed meeting them and learning about their business. And then, we overnight them a sample of Callahan coffee. They might take Monday off to rest after the trade show, so by the time they come in Tuesday, they've got a gift box from Callahan waiting for them on their desk. *That's* what I call being resourceful."

Just then, Angie came rushing around the corner, looking somewhat frantic. "Jasmine!" she cried. "Channel 4 just called. They had to reshuffle some things in their lineup. They want to know if they can send their field reporter *today*. Just before noon. Like, in three hours."

Jasmine's eyes widened.

"What's this about?" Max asked.

Angie turned to him. "You know Tanner Patrick on the six o'clock news? The guy who does the on-location stories? We arranged for him to come to Callahan and be a 'Roaster for a Day.' Jasmine was going to give the crew the special Callahan tour, and they were going to put together a three-minute spot that would really show off Callahan. But it wasn't scheduled for a couple more weeks. And the Design Department had this great idea to put his face on some labels and put it on the coffee, so it would look like it was 'Tanner Patrick's Special Roast.' But now there's no way they'll have time."

Jasmine furrowed her brow, thinking. "Remember what Doug used to say?" she asked. "If I had a million dollars sitting here in front of you ... could you do it then?"

Angie grinned. "Yeah, I remember. Okay—I think it's at least worth a shot, don't you? If we don't get the labels done in time, we can still do the tour and the roasting stuff."

"Exactly," said Jasmine. She turned to Max. "Looks like we're going to be on TV tonight. Good thing you wore a nice shirt!" she joked, laughing.

"I'll call them back and say it's a go," Angie said. "Jasmine, think you can convince the Design Department to pull this off?"

"I'm on it."

For the next few hours, Max witnessed a team of people pull together, work hard, and turn out a beautiful product—all without stressing or losing faith in each other. They put their minds and creativity together, and that evening, as Max watched Tanner Patrick laughingly hold up 'Tanner Patrick's Special Roast' on the evening news, he had to agree with the Callahan perspective: With the right mind-set, nothing is impossible.

• • •

CORE VALUE #3

Be Creative and Resourceful.

At Callahan creativity and resourcefulness are everywhere. You see it in our branding, the way we solve problems, and how we work every day. We believe that with the right mindset, there is always a way and nothing is impossible.

CHAPTER FOUR

CORE VALUE #4
Optimize Our Financial Resources

A budget is telling your money where to go instead of wondering where it went.
—**Dave Ramsey**

"I CAN'T make heads or tails of any of this," Max said, gesturing at the pile of documents spread over the small surface of his rolling desk. His laptop was balanced precariously at the corner of the desk, several more documents and spreadsheets open on its screen.

Max had been looking at Callahan budgets all morning. He'd gone back ten years to get a sense of the company's history and begun working his way forward, looking at how the company had evolved and grown. The trouble was, he couldn't get beyond a very simple question—a question so simple, so basic, so "Business 101" that he couldn't bring himself to ask for clarification.

And so he'd spent hours going in circles, clicking back and forth between spreadsheets, printing out documents so he could lay them across his desk and look at more columns at once ... and still he hadn't figured it out. He had no idea what he was looking at.

The question was: Where did the numbers at the start of each year come from?

When Max compared a budget from any given year to that of the next year, it looked to him like none of the figures carried over. A particular department might be allotted $50,000 one year and only $35,000 the next—regardless of whether it had underspent. Another department might be allotted $50,000 one year and $80,000 the next—even if it hadn't overspent.

Finally, feeling foolish and frustrated, Max had wheeled his little desk out of his quiet corner of the Sales Department and into the office of the CFO, Randall Morgan.

Randall was a slender, soft-spoken man in his mid-fifties. He had an easy, relaxed smile and an air of quiet competence—the kind of guy you'd be glad to have around in a crisis. And that was a good thing, since, in Max's mind, Callahan's current loss of revenue more or less qualified as a "crisis." Max had gotten to know Randall during his interview process, and was looking forward to relying on him to help work out a plan for getting Callahan back on track. They got along well, and they seemed to share a straightforward, pragmatic approach to management—which was why Max felt baffled about the budgets now. He couldn't imagine Randall doing something as fundamental as budgeting without a tried-and-true method.

"I can't figure out how you guys are coming up with these projections," Max said. "Sometimes I see consistency from year to year, but more often than not, I can't find a pattern here. Why aren't you carrying over one year's spending as the next year's projected spending?"

Randall stood over the little rolling desk, hands loosely slung in his pockets, looking down at the mess of spreadsheets. "Well, the simple answer is that that doesn't actually make a whole lot of sense," he said.

Max waited for Randall to explain, trying to put on a patient expression. By this time, he'd been at Callahan long enough to know that this was not your typical company and that people were going to have ways of doing things that surprised him. So far those surprises had all turned out to be good ones—but that didn't mean the company wasn't in a difficult situation. Randall better have a good explanation for whatever was going on here.

"When we're writing a new budget for the next year," Randall continued, "we start at zero. We don't just ask ourselves, 'What did we spend last year?' and then paint by numbers accordingly. We ask ourselves, 'What do we need to accomplish our goals?' "

Max was taken aback. It wasn't that he'd never heard of writing a budget that way before, but he'd never actually come across it in practice at any of the companies where he'd worked. It just wasn't the standard procedure.

Clearly, Randall could see his hesitation. "It's an extremely careful process," he said, almost reassuringly. "We don't pull numbers out of thin air. In fact, we do the opposite. We rely on a solid guiding principle, which is Core Value number four ...

Optimize Our Financial Resources.

The idea behind it is that there's a right number when it comes to spending. You can spend too much, of course. But you can also spend too little. And we're always searching for that sweet spot—that optimal number."

"Okay ..." Max said. It sounded good in theory. "So how do you find it?"

"The previous year's numbers are helpful, for sure,"

Randall said, "but much more important are our goals for the new year. So, each year, the Callahan directors and upper-level managers go off-site for a three-day retreat, and we hash out those goals. And then we determine what's needed to achieve those goals, whether that means cutting back or beefing up spending."

"How do you keep a cap on things?" Max asked, still not convinced. "It sounds like you could just spend without limit."

"Well," Randall said, "I think there's actually *more* risk of that when you base projections on the previous year. You'll run into a lot of companies where department managers do a lot of haphazard, unfocused spending in the last month of the fiscal year because they want to spend all their budget so they'll get the same amount the next year."

Max paused. Randall had an excellent point there. It was something he'd struggled with repeatedly: Getting managers to spend any remaining money in a forward-thinking way, a way that would yield returns down the road instead of just getting rid of the extra cash. Too often, as the end of a fiscal year loomed, he'd come across contract workers sitting around twiddling their thumbs or storage closets filled with Post-It notes—all kinds of useless spending that accomplished nothing but meeting the budget.

"And there's a lot of accountability for upper-level managers," Randall continued. "Our bonuses are based on whether or not we meet our budgets. If we don't make the budget, we get zero. But that's really just a different way of saying that if we don't meet our goals, we get zero. We have to work together, always reevaluating what that optimal number is. So take this year, for example. We've had a setback, so maybe that means we invest more in sales to get back on track—and at the same time, we don't just throw cash at it so that sales gets inefficient and unfocused."

Max sat back and folded his arms. It was certainly an unorthodox approach, but he liked the challenge it created. It was almost like a new puzzle with each new budget. Every year, Callahan had a fresh opportunity to strategize, to think about possibilities for the future as if it were a brand-new company rather than just chugging along on its old, decades-long momentum.

"I kind of like it ..." Max said slowly. "It reminds me of when I was fresh out of business school and ready to take on anything. It's like Callahan gets to renew the entrepreneurial spirit every single year."

"Exactly!" Randall agreed, nodding enthusiastically. "It's easy to pay lip service to optimizing resources, but it's a different story entirely when you really *have* to because you're starting from zero."

"Okay, then here's my next question," Max said, bringing up the current year's budget on his laptop screen. "I was thinking about how we might reinvest in sales, and I wanted to see how much wiggle room we have. But I can't seem to find anything about our lines of credit here. Do you have those tracked separately?"

"We don't have them."

Max stared at Randall, uncomprehending. "What do you mean? You're not keeping track of Callahan's credit? How do you know how much we owe?"

"I mean we don't have lines of credit," Randall said.

"What?"

"Callahan is a debt-free company. We have no lines of credit. We don't even give our sales reps credit cards for expenses—they use prepaid debit cards when they're out of town." Randall said this so nonchalantly that Max had to take a moment to get his brain around it.

"But ... we've got over seventy employees. We're operating across the United States. I'm missing something here. How on earth can we operate without borrowing?"

"The more important question would be 'How would we operate if we *did* borrow?' " Randall said. "We'd be a lot less nimble, that's for sure." He riffled through some of the printed spreadsheets on the rolling desk and finally pulled one out. "See this from two years ago?" He pointed to a new line item that had been added to the year's projected spending: "Ronzoni's Coffee Roasters," it read.

"Doug might have mentioned this to you," Randall went on. "This was one of our smaller competitors. They ran into some financial trouble, and it opened up an opportunity for us—but we needed to move fast. Because we were debt-free, we were able to quickly take advantage of that opportunity, and we bought Ronzoni's outright, with cash. That's what being debt-free means to us. It gives us the maneuverability of a much smaller company."

"You know this is going to make our current situation really tough," Max said. "I'm not sure how we can account for a 20 percent loss of revenue without borrowing."

"We can," Randall said, confidently. "We've operated this way since the beginning, and we've met tougher challenges before. I'd even argue that right now more than ever, we can't afford debt. Again, there's an optimal number for every situation. I think the way we're going to get our revenue back on track isn't by borrowing what we don't have, but by cashing in on what we do have—the company's reputation and quality. And I know you and Jasmine have been working hard on leveraging those in our favor." Here he was clearly alluding to the potential deal with Waterbury Coffeehouses.

Max drummed his fingers on the table. "Listen, I've been really impressed with what I've seen around here," he said. "So I'm willing to give this idea the benefit of the doubt. Again—it's not what I'm used to, but it seems like you guys have a penchant for surprising me. Let's give it some more time to see what happens with Waterbury, and then we'll talk about it again."

Randall nodded, a knowing smile beginning to spread across his face. "Absolutely," he said, "but I have a feeling we won't need to."

· · ·

CORE VALUE #4

Optimize Our Financial Resources.

We approach financial management with the attitude that there is a right number when it comes to spending. We will accomplish our goals by spending not too much or too little, but the correct amount to complete our objectives.

CHAPTER FIVE

CORE VALUE #5

Never Stop Learning and Growing

The more that you read, the more things you will know. The more that you learn, the more places you'll go.
—Dr. Seuss

AS MAX was leaving Randall's office with his rolling desk, Rhonda came excitedly down the hall, walking so quickly she was almost running.

"It's done! Your office is done!" she called as soon as she was in earshot. "The electrician is finished; the drywall is set; the paint is dry. It still kind of smells like paint, but I opened the windows. I got Ted to bring in your new desk and some filing cabinets and shelving. It's all ready."

Before Max had a chance to reply, Rhonda motioned for him to follow her and began leading the way back up the hall toward his office. Max realized that he probably wouldn't need his rolling desk anymore, but not knowing where else to put it, he wheeled it along behind her and into the CEO's office through the open door.

He had to admit, it looked great. The electrician had installed soft, discreet overhead lighting, and Ted had set up a brand-new executive desk facing the door of the office. Its dark, polished wood gleamed in the sunlight streaming through the windows.

At the sight of that large, solid, immovable desk, a strange idea struck Max out of the blue.

"Rhonda, this is fantastic," he said. "Really, it is. I'm so grateful for the work you put into organizing this, and I can't wait to 'move in,' so to speak. But—I just had an idea. I mean, so far, I've been working in the reception area, the Delivery Department, the Sales Department, and even in Randall's office, all sort of by accident. But in every place, I've learned so much. Everybody has made me look at Callahan in a new, clearer way—and frankly, I'm starting to think about business in general differently, too."

Rhonda was listening patiently, but Max couldn't help feeling a little awkward about his sudden idea as he went on. "It seems like I should know Callahan as well as

Doug did, and I'm starting to think this little desk"—he gestured down at the rolling desk before him—"might be a good tool. What if I keep it awhile and use it to visit some more of Callahan's departments before I really settle into this office?"

Max was worried he sounded like a lunatic, but Rhonda grinned. "I think that's a great idea." She cocked her head playfully. "Have you been studying the Core Values?"

"What do you mean?"

"Well, it sounds like your idea is right in line with Core Value number five ...

Never Stop Learning and Growing.

It's exactly the kind of curious, creative attitude Doug was always encouraging. No wonder he thought you'd fit right in here."

Max laughed. "Yeah, Doug did say he thought Callahan and I were a great match for each other. I don't think I ever could have guessed how, though. And that's why I want to keep exploring around the company. Callahan employees keep surprising me—I want to know what's next."

"Hey, here's an idea for a start," Rhonda said. "I've been working on the logistics for the upcoming Origin Trip ..."

This was something Max was really excited about. Years ago, Doug had started a tradition. Every year, Callahan would send its CEO, its Director of Coffee, some salespeople, and a few select customers to visit some of the farms Callahan bought from in one of the coffee-growing regions. In a few months, Max would be headed to El Salvador with many of his colleagues—it would be his first trip to Central America.

When Doug first designed the trips, the idea he had in mind was to create connections among Callahan, its customers, and the farmers who produced the coffee. And bringing along long-standing Callahan customers helped ensure the knowledge and the sense of connection got passed down to the coffeehouses that ultimately sold the coffee. Each trip stirred up a lot of curiosity and passion in the customers, and it introduced them to new types of coffees they might want to incorporate into their menus.

The exchange of ideas and information was also a two-way street. Doug had told Max about bringing roasted Callahan coffee to a grower, specially packaged in a Callahan bags. It was the first time the grower had seen his coffee roasted, prepared, and packaged. The experience was extremely rewarding for everyone on both sides of coffee production. It was a way of building "coffee culture" in a profound, human context.

"You know the trip is coming up," Rhonda said. "And we're going to be sending one of our employees, Dean Trumbell, who works in Packaging, along with you. Doug picked him before he retired, but I haven't had a chance to deliver the good news yet. If you want to, you could do it—it would be a great excuse to take your desk to the Packaging Department and hang out there for a while."

"Wait, slow down," Max said. "I'm not sure if I remember Dean. Why did Doug want him to go to El Salvador if he's a packager? Does he have something to do with buying?"

"Nothing at all—that's the point!" Rhonda exclaimed.

"Ah, another one of Callahan's mysteries ..." Max said, half teasing but honestly bewildered. "Please enlighten me."

"Every year, Doug would pick an additional employee to go on the Origin Trip—*any* employee, from *any* department, but it had to be someone who wouldn't be going on the trip otherwise. He'd pick that person based on their enthusiasm for coffee and their initiative to educate themselves about it."

"How did he know who had enthusiasm and initiative?" Max asked. "Is there some kind of contest?"

"No," Rhonda said. "That's what's really fantastic about it. You know about our weekly coffee tastings, right?"

"Yeah," Max said. "I'm excited to attend my first one tomorrow."

"So you know they're not required," Rhonda continued. "It's a fun opportunity for employees to train their palates and learn about the subtleties of coffee's flavors—just like a wine tasting. They get an idea of how to recognize and describe the taste of different coffees. But it's entirely voluntary. Whoever gets picked for an Origin Trip is usually one of the employees who make it a point to come to tastings.

"And we have other classes about coffee we offer from time to time, like the Cup of Knowledge. That's where employees can learn about the agricultural side of production—like harvesting and processing. We've given classes on everything from customer service to espresso extraction. It's all about developing our employees' skills and recognition of just how complex and fascinating coffee can be. It really builds an environment where people know a lot about coffee—and care about it.

"There are more creative employee development opportunities thrown in there, too. For example ... have you seen our *Callahan Latte Art Book*?"

Max cringed. "Ugh," he said, a joking smile creeping across his face. "I've been dreading when someone would bring that up. Angie showed it to me last week. I was hoping I could get out of it undetected!"

Rhonda laughed. "That's what I used to think, too, but it's actually a lot of fun! I'm so glad I learned how to do it."

The *Callahan Latte Art Book* was a big coffee-table book that Max had found displayed in the reception area. As he flipped through its pages, he saw large, glossy photos of lattes—each one displaying "latte art," a design made with a blended texture of espresso and steamed milk. Some had perfect heart-shaped layers of foamed milk, others intricate rosettas, which looked like the leaves of ferns. Many weren't exactly what you'd call "perfect," but Max could see that each latte had been carefully prepared.

When Max asked Angie about the book, she explained to him that every two years, all the Callahan employees—again, every single one, from the roasters to the marketing personnel—took a class on how to create latte art. Some of the employees who had been baristas were already old hands, but others never really got many chances to play with an espresso machine—so it was an opportunity to practice a new, different skill. They could go as in-depth with it as they wanted, but everyone had to at least learn the basics. And then Callahan created a book with photos of everyone's latte art and a caption with their name and position in the company.

"I don't think you understand, Rhonda," Max said, laughingly. "I am the most artistically challenged human being on the planet. My pour is going to be pathetic."

"I was worried about mine, too!" Rhonda exclaimed. "But you'll get the hang of it. And even if it's not perfect, you'll be in good company. The point is that we're all in this together and we all get to know something special about coffee. There isn't an employee here who's just in it for the paycheck—we chose Callahan because we have passion for the industry. And Callahan cares about developing and rewarding that passion.

"Besides," she said slyly, "you've got several months before we make the next book, so start studying now."

Max couldn't help smiling. He already knew he'd have to take this one on the chin and let himself go down in history as the coffee company CEO who couldn't pour latte art.

"Okay," Max said, "back to the matter at hand. Dean Trumbell gets a trip to El Salvador because he's curious about coffee?"

"That's right," said Rhonda.

"I don't know if I get it. Why does a packager need to know how coffee is grown?"

"I thought you might say that. I wondered about it when I first started here, too, to be honest. But ... well, let's just say a little experience had me convinced. Something tells me that if you meet Dean, you'll start to understand."

Max shrugged willingly. "It can't hurt. I'll give it a try."

As he made his way to the warehouse where the Packaging Department was, Max thought to himself that the cost of Dean's trip was probably already budgeted, so there was no harm going ahead with it. But this particular expense was one that he'd have to have a tough talk with Randall about when they started considering next year. He was absolutely in favor of rewarding enthusiastic employees, but maybe a gift card to a local coffeehouse could make the same statement.

Max wheeled his desk into the center of the large, open floor space of the Packaging Department, where employees were busy transferring whole-bean and ground coffee from large metal hoppers into Callahan packaging for distribution. For a moment, Max thought about standing on his rolling desk to make his grand announcement—but then he looked down at its wobbly wheels and thought better of it. Instead, he rapped loudly on the desk with his knuckles.

"Attention, everyone! Is Dean Trumbell present?" he called in a stern voice.

A wiry young man with black-frame glasses stepped forward, still holding a bag of coffee and looking nervous.

"Mr. Trumbell," Max said, "your reputation precedes you. I've heard that you, sir, are a coffee aficionado, and in honor of your curiosity and your commitment to learning about Callahan's product, we're sending you on this year's Origin Trip to El Salvador!"

Rhonda had prepared a folder for Dean with his trip itinerary and travel documents. Max handed the folder over and shook Dean's hand as the rest of the packagers broke into applause and cheers.

"Wow!" Dean said. "I—I'm totally surprised. I've only been working here a little over a year."

"Oh yeah? What brought you to Callahan?" asked Max.

"I just really like coffee," Dean said. "I was a barista,

too, but Callahan seemed like a more stable job now that I'm done with school. And there are benefits and a chance to move up."

"That's true," Max said. "And you've already distinguished yourself. Doug was really impressed with you, which is why he picked you for the trip. Tell me about your year here. What have you enjoyed the most?"

"What's great," Dean answered, "is that I get a chance here to understand how coffee is made. I already knew something about different coffee brewing methods from working at a coffee shop, but here I get to see the whole process. But it's not just the coffee, it's that there are all kinds of ways I can keep learning at Callahan—about coffee and about business."

"How so?" asked Max, starting to see why Doug had taken note of this young man's initiative.

Dean reached into his back pocket and pulled out a paperback copy of the Dale Carnegie classic *How to Win Friends and Influence People*. "Well, for example, I picked this up at the Callahan library. As soon as I started working here, I heard people talking about this reading program Doug started."

"Yeah, I just got a look at the library the other day," Max said, suddenly feeling guilty that he had jotted down the Callahan Reading Program as a possible expense to cut. Doug had created a library room where employees could share books and then write short reviews and summaries of them on an online forum. As an added incentive to keep employees challenging themselves, Callahan paid them fifteen cents per page that they read, up to $200 a year. Now, as Max heard the excitement in Dean's voice, he was starting to understand the reasoning behind the Reading Program.

"There are a lot of business and personal development books in the library—I mean, of course, since Callahan is a growing business," Dean said. "And I'm really getting a lot out of them. My grandfather used to quote Harry Truman: 'Not all readers become leaders. But all leaders must be readers.' Doug put the same quote on the wall of the library. So that made me feel like I was on the right track.

"I like working hands-on with the coffee right now. But maybe someday I'll want to move to the Sales or Marketing Department. I mean, anything's possible. Who knows what I'll learn in El Salvador, right?" Dean broke into a broad grin.

Max returned the smile. "I hope you get a lot out of the trip, Dean," he said. And he really meant it. He could see exactly why Doug had decided that initiatives that kept employees learning and growing were essential to Callahan.

• • •

CORE VALUE #5

Never Stop Learning and Growing.

We want everybody to take on an attitude of lifelong learning. This can be done through books, classes, and stimulating conversations. This is not just about coffee; it is about developing and growing to become your own best self.

Chapter Six

CORE VALUE #6
Embrace Change and Reevaluate Systems

If you do not change direction, you may end up where you are heading.
—Lao Tzu

"Hey, I heard you've been camping out in different departments," a voice called out as Max was finishing his conversation with Dean Trumbell about the upcoming Origin Trip. "How would you like to stick around in Packaging and find out what we do all day?"

Max turned to see Arthur Brooks, the manager of the Packaging Department. Arthur was a broad-shouldered, bald fellow with a thick, black goatee. He looked like he'd be at home driving a big rig. Max extended his hand in greeting.

"Sounds great," he told Arthur. "I'll just set up my desk over here against the wall."

"Well, that would be just fine. But I was actually going to suggest you put it right there." Arthur pointed across the Packaging room floor to a massive steel machine. It was tall, with stairs leading up one side to a platform where an employee was loading coffee through a funnel. At the base of the machine, a conveyor belt released bags of coffee that two more employees were picking up and stacking neatly into perfect rows on a rolling hopper.

"What on earth is that?" Max asked. "It looks like an industrial trash compactor."

"It bags coffee!" Arthur said. "Not only does it *bag* the coffee ... it actually makes the bags too."

Max raised an eyebrow. "That's pretty cool," he said.

Max followed Arthur toward the machine. "We load the machine with rolls of film," Arthur explained, "and the film gets made into a bag, and then the bag gets filled with coffee based on weights that we input into the system." Arthur patted the side of the machine as he might pat the flank of a beloved horse.

Max looked around. Besides the rolling hopper where employees were loading the coffee bags, he didn't see any other storage space. Pointing at the single hopper, he asked Arthur, "Is that all our inventory? I thought we had a great deal more than that."

"Well, of course there's a whole lot more raw beans ready for the roasting process," Arthur said. "But that's all the roasted coffee we've got for today. We'll start packaging tomorrow's coffee in the morning—right after it's finished roasting."

"You mean we don't inventory our coffee? Keep some extra on hand a bit ahead of time?"

"Of course not. We move it fresh every day."

"But doesn't it keep just fine for a little while?"

Arthur gave Max a sly grin. "That's what our competitors say," he said. "We've got a different approach to coffee around here."

Max raised his eyebrows, impressed. "Was this one of Doug's rogue ideas?"

Arthur chuckled. "How'd you guess? But actually, it wasn't something he came up with early on. For most of our history, we did stock coffee just like everyone else. But then Doug started asking, 'Why?' There really is a difference between coffee that has been stored and coffee that's fresh. We could all taste it. So Doug started asking, 'Why are we settling? Just because everyone else does it?'"

"So when did you make the change?"

"It's been about six years. And I tell you what, none of

us would ever go back," Arthur said. "But in the beginning, it wasn't an easy switch."

"How do you mean?" Max asked. "Seems like it's the right idea for a company founded on quality."

"Well, absolutely. But we had whole system." Arthur indicated the far wall where a large chart was displayed. "That's the Packaging Chart," he explained. "It helps us sort out what coffee needs to get packaged for tomorrow's deliveries. You can see there are a lot of different roasts and blends to keep track of, a lot of different weights. So the team had a strong, efficient system for keeping all that organized.

"We were roasting coffee ahead of time and keeping an inventory. As the customers would place an order, we'd pull the coffee off the shelf. Some of the bags would be older than others, of course, but it worked.

"Then Doug and I sat down and had a talk about what we were doing. And the two of us agreed we really needed to make a major switch to completely on-demand roasting. Now we only roast the coffee after a customer calls, so we have the ultimate freshness.

"People weren't thrilled about it. It wasn't just a daunting change for the roasters and packagers. Our business advisors and some of our board members were pretty skittish too. They all thought that kind of overhaul would be too disruptive. But we were willing to work hard to make it work. We all pulled together to reinvent our process."

Max nodded. "Change can definitely be daunting, especially when things are going well enough as they are."

"It's true," Arthur agreed. "But here at Callahan we're constantly trying to avoid falling into the trap of complacency. Just because everything appears to be working fine doesn't mean it couldn't stand a little reevaluation. If you take a second look at it, and you can't think of a single way to improve things—fine. But odds are, there's always room for improvement. So, when Doug proposed the new roasting and packaging process, I wanted to give the idea the consideration it deserved. And we decided together that it was a change that would improve quality—and even efficiency too—and pay for itself over the long term."

"So you're always considering new approaches even if you don't necessarily feel that Callahan is in need of a new system?" Max wanted to know.

"Of course!" Arthur said. "How would I know if we

needed to change if I didn't periodically reevaluate what's in place? Let me give you an example ... This is an old story, but a good one.

"Once upon a time, a young couple was getting dinner together, and the husband saw his wife slice off the end of the ham before she put it in the pan.

" 'Why did you do that?' he asked his wife.

" 'Oh,' the wife said, 'this is just how my mom taught me to roast a ham.'

"But then she got to thinking about it herself, so the next time she saw her mother, she asked her why she had taught her to cut off the end of the ham.

" 'Well, that's how your grandmother taught me to do it,' the mother answered.

"Again, the wife was perplexed. So she stopped in at her grandmother's house.

" 'Why did you teach Mom to cut off the end of the ham before putting it in the pan?' she asked.

"Her grandmother looked at her quizzically. 'Well ... when your grandfather and I were younger, we only had this one little pan.' She pulled an old pan out of the cabinet. 'I had to slice the ham so it would fit. But now I have a much better, much bigger roasting pan. In fact, I bought you the same one as your wedding present.' "

Max laughed out loud. "I guess it doesn't make sense to just keep doing things blindly because it's the way it's always been done. You've got to ask why."

"Exactly!" Arthur said. "Doug was of the mind that there's no stable state in business. You're either growing or you're shrinking; there's no such thing as staying the same. And that's why we have Core Value number six ...

Embrace Change and Reevaluate Systems.

It's not about changing for change's sake, of course. It's about constantly striving to improve—because if you're not, then you're slipping behind."

"I agree on that point," Max said. "Companies that aren't constantly innovating aren't going to stay in business. But not everybody can get on board with reevaluating. How do you deal with pushback when you change up the way things have always been done?"

"That's a tough one," Arthur said. "I mean, I think Doug cultivated the community here at Callahan very carefully, so that people really do believe in the Core Values and embrace them. But every now and then you'll find that someone seems to be on board with the company culture ... but is actually finding ways to hold back.

"Doug had a pretty rough situation not too long ago with an employee we'd had for quite some time—ten years. Every time a new innovation was proposed, he would be the first to list everything that was wrong with the idea and why it wouldn't work, even before we had tried it.

"Eventually, Doug sat down with him and pointed this out. He showed this fellow how his attitude was keeping things from moving forward, and he asked him to try being more open-minded. If an idea comes up and there are cons, well, we can talk about them—but if the idea has enough pros, we might as well give it a shot. If it still doesn't work, then we'll learn from that and move on.

"So Doug gave this guy a chance to try that approach ... and he just couldn't get it into his system. Still, he was the naysayer. Finally, Doug made the hard decision to let him go. That's how important culture fit is around here. Not that we're looking for a bunch of clones and yes-men—far from it. Disagreement can be productive. But we need people who are willing to see possibilities and to welcome change if it can be good for the company, if it can help us move forward."

Max nodded slowly. He couldn't disagree with Doug's decision in that case.

"In fact," Arthur went on, "Doug cared so much about Core Value number six that every year, he would give out the Doug Thompson Impactful Change Award. It was the only award he gave out, and it went to an employee who understood that Callahan's success depends on constant change. He'd look for an employee who was always thinking of ways to improve processes, to become more efficient, or to solve problems creatively. The award could go to any employee in any department. It was just another way of reinforcing how much we need to always be looking critically at what we're doing and asking, 'Is this still the best way?'"

"Well, that's one thing I *don't* want to change!" Max said, smiling. "I'll definitely continue to give that award."

Arthur chuckled. "I'm glad to hear it. If you ask me, Core Value number six is one of the most important values. It's why I know Callahan is going to be okay."

As Arthur went back to his work in the Packaging Department office, Max sat down at his little rolling desk. "It's why I know Callahan is going to be okay," he heard Arthur's voice in his head again.

Something was beginning to brew for Max. All along, he had been thinking of Callahan's 20 percent loss of revenue as a serious problem. But Core Value number six had gotten him thinking. In adversity, there is always opportunity. Maybe this was a chance for Callahan to reevaluate and to improve how it was functioning as a company. Not in the ways that Max was used to—by slashing head count and reducing the company's production. Instead, maybe there was a way to think about creating real, galvanizing change that was still in line with the Core Values Callahan had been built upon.

Max drummed his fingers on the surface of the desk. He knew he still had a lot to learn about Callahan—but he was starting to see that everything he was learning was leading toward something. Something he couldn't quite envision yet—but something he would never have anticipated before that little rolling desk came along and started all these new ideas in motion.

• • •

CORE VALUE #6

Embrace Change and Reevaluate Systems.

Change happens. Companies evolve. The actions that got us to where we are today aren't necessarily the same actions that will take us to tomorrow. We will strive to be unique and never do things because "that's the way we have always done them." We relentlessly create and refine systems to maximize our efficiency and effectiveness.

Chapter Seven

CORE VALUE #7
Communicate Clearly and Openly

The single biggest problem with communication is the illusion that it has taken place.
—George Bernard Shaw

MAX ARRIVED at Callahan the next morning prepared to flip a coin to decide where his rolling desk would take him next. He knew he wanted to keep learning from Callahan's employees, but he'd also seen enough by now to know that it was impossible to predict what new ideas they would toss at him next. So he was going to let fate decide.

And then Lisa Farber headed him off at the pass.

"Max!" she called just as he came through the front door of the reception area. "I hear you need a place to park your desk. Come to HR."

Well, if that wasn't fate intervening, Max didn't know what was.

"Okay then," he agreed. "Let me just get the desk out of my office"—the absurdity of this statement was not lost on him—"and I'll meet you there."

When he arrived at the small cluster of desks in the open office space where Lisa, the Human Resources manager, worked with two administrative assistants, Max was excited to see what made Lisa so eager.

"Okay," he said, "if HR is anything like the other Callahan departments I've visited, I know I've got a lot to learn here. But tell me why you wanted me to stop by HR."

"Because HR deals with human beings," Lisa said, "and human beings are Callahan's reason for being. Remember our mission statement? *Help people, make friends, have fun.* That's it. I want you to get to know the lifeblood of this organization."

Max grinned. "It's about time," he said. "So how did Callahan end up with such a people-centered mission statement, anyway?"

"Well, from the beginning," Lisa said, "Callahan has been about people with passion doing everything they can to turn that passion into reality. Doug was passionate about the business, and he wanted to find people who were equally passionate. Did you know that Doug actually slept at Callahan's first facility when he opened it two decades ago?"

"No, I didn't!" Max said, amazed. "He didn't mention that when he told me about founding the company."

"Well, he literally had nothing," Lisa said. "He used every last scrap of his money to start the business—to lease a building and buy the bare minimum, used roasting equipment to get started. He had just gotten a divorce, and Callahan was all that he had in his life. He poured his heart into it. He actually slept in the first Callahan building for a year before things took off and he started making enough profit to actually get a real place to live."

"That's real dedication," Max said.

"Doug told me that story when he interviewed me for this position," Lisa said, "and I knew right away that I wanted this job more than anything. This isn't just a company; it's a community. And a lot of that, in the beginning, had to do with Doug's initiative, and the way he built the company around its people."

Lisa paused. "Maybe you've heard Tony Robbins tell this story before ... about the pastor and his sermon?"

"No, tell me."

"Well, there was a pastor who kept delivering the same sermon every Sunday. Weeks went by, and every

Sunday morning, he said the exact same thing, with the exact same lesson. Finally, some of the elder members of the parish waited for him after services and—respectfully, gently—let him know that he was repeating himself.

"The pastor just smiled. And he said, 'I'm glad you noticed it was the same sermon. And I plan to keep delivering it until you actually hear it. I'll keep preaching this sermon until you actually do what it calls on you to do.' "

"Hmm," said Max. "He had his way of making his point. But what does that have to do with Doug? Did he like to repeat himself?"

Lisa laughed. "I think that story is Tony Robbins reminding us to really listen and incorporate what we're hearing into meaningful action. We're quick to say, 'I know. I've heard that one over and over,' but if you actually look at what we're *doing* ... it's as if we haven't heard a thing.

"And I think Doug liked that story because it was a good reminder for him. I think this was the area where he struggled the most."

Max was silent for a moment. He certainly hadn't expected that. All of Callahan's employees thus far had been presenting Doug Thompson, their former CEO, as an almost mythic figure—brilliant and innovative *and* fun-loving. And here was Lisa telling him that Doug had an Achilles' heel.

"What it comes down to, I think," Lisa continued, "is Callahan's Core Value number seven ...

Communicate Clearly and Openly.

It's the Core Value that we struggle with the most. It's the one we talk about the most, too—probably because it's our biggest challenge. And I think that's natural. In any organization or group of people—in any family even—most problems boil down to issues of communication. It's hard to master. Maybe you don't ever even master it. It's something that you have to continually cultivate."

Max was intrigued. "So what was Doug's approach to cultivating communication?" he asked.

"He believed that leadership needed to model the kind of open, effective communication that he wanted to see throughout the rest of the organization. I've heard him quote Dave Ramsey: 'Don't be a mushroom communicator, leaving your people in the dark and feeding them manure.'

"Instead, he wanted leadership to be vulnerable. Completely open and not secretive. So every year, he would give out a survey, asking *all* of the employees, 'How can I be a better leader?'"

"Seriously?" Max asked. "Wasn't that just opening himself up to a lot of complaining and criticism?"

"Actually, you'd be surprised how productive it was," Lisa said. "I'm sure that if he just passed out the survey and then ignored the feedback, it *would* end up just being a lot of whining. But because people knew that Doug's attitude was to be completely accepting of criticism, they could be very honest. They knew that he wouldn't get defensive; instead he would make changes."

"It's a pretty incredible idea," Max said, making a mental note to himself to ask Rhonda to check her files for a copy of the survey. "If Doug was that open to constructive criticism and ready to keep improving himself, it seems like it would have to influence the rest of the company culture."

"That was the idea," Lisa said. "And I think it really worked. I've always thought of Callahan as a place where people aren't afraid of sharing. We've built trusting relationships so that people can speak their minds without fear of leaving a meeting feeling hurt or having some kind of internal conflict hinder their performance. And if there was a conflict that just wasn't getting anywhere, Doug would sometimes literally take the employees involved to the conference room, close the door, and tell them, 'Don't come out until you've worked this out.'"

"Wow," Max said. "But wait a minute ... that kind of vulnerability just isn't going to work for everyone. I mean, I'm sure to a certain extent it can be learned and people can get better at it—but you've probably also got to be careful in the hiring process and make sure that you're choosing people who will be open to that kind of environment."

"I'm glad you said that!" Lisa said. "That's the main thing I wanted to show you. I'm sure you remember when Doug first contacted you about taking over, he sent you the Callahan 22."

"Of course," Max said. "How could I forget?" Doug had sent him a series of twenty-two questions. It was clearly a hiring questionnaire that went to all levels of prospective employees; Max couldn't remember filling out an application of that kind since long before he had moved up to executive level positions. But he liked Doug and found the questions entertaining, so he obliged.

Some of them were fairly standard fare for a prospective employee, like, "Describe a weakness of a past
supervisor and how you dealt with them." And some
were a little more outside the box: "What are the last
three books you read?" and "What's the most creative
thing you've done in the last five months?"

"Well, every new employee gets the Callahan 22,"
Lisa told him.

"*Every* new employee?" Max asked. "Even, say, the
delivery drivers?"

"Yup. Everyone. We're all part of the same company.
So it's a way of getting a sense of a person's personality.
Will they fit in with the Callahan team?"

"Wait, wait, wait," Max said. "I have a lot of questions. But first of all: Why twenty-two? Why not twenty?
Or ten for that matter?"

Lisa laughed. "Just more of Callahan having fun," she
said with a grin. "You've noticed the number twenty-two
around here, right?"

"I mean ... sure, the big '22' painted on the front hallway wall, you mean?"

Lisa couldn't suppress an amused giggle. "That's the
only one you've seen?" she asked, her voice in mock
astonishment. "It's everywhere! It's like our personal

Callahan *Where's Waldo* game. It's in all of our packaging and marketing materials. Look closer. You'll see a '22' on all of our cups, bags, posters." She paused. "Also ... count the letters in 'Callahan Coffee Roasters.' "

Max did, counting them out on his fingers. Twenty-two letters.

"I mean, it's not like Doug named it with twenty-two letters on purpose," Lisa said quickly. "But once he figured out that it did have twenty-two letters, you can bet he was pleased."

Max could not have felt sillier. Once again, he reminded himself, he had to remember that Callahan was not your typical Company, Inc., and that he needed to loosen up a little and learn to play by its rules. He would definitely be scouring the building for twenty-twos from now on.

"So is that just a lucky number or something?" he asked.

"I guess you could say that," Lisa said. "Doug's birthday is 2/22. And he was a fan of a basketball player who was number 22. It just kept cropping up, so he thought it was fun. And that's why the cornerstone of our hiring process is the Callahan 22."

"So what does the Callahan 22 really do for you?"

Max wanted to know. "I get that it gives you a sense of who an applicant is. But in terms of hiring—what does it tell you about performance?"

"Well, for us, job performance is bound up in fitting with the company culture. It sounds strange, but our goal is to make it hard to get a job here—at any level, and even to make lateral moves within the company. At every interview, for any position, there are several leadership people present."

Max was hesitant. "It sounds like you might scare prospective employees away."

"I think it's the opposite. I think we attract exactly the kind of employees we want. It's not about placing a warm body in the job; it's about completing the full picture that is Callahan. We've even been willing, in the past, to pay a little extra in overtime until we're able to find the right fit."

"So what's the track record? Does it work?"

Lisa smiled. "We have a little test for that. This is a modified version of an idea Doug got from Tony Hsieh at Zappos. After an employee's first ninety days, we sit them down for a review. That's typical, of course—most companies do that. But at that review, we say to them, 'Here's a check for $2,222.22—there's twenty-two coming into play again!—'Here's the check. If you want to quit now, it's yours.' No one has ever taken it. And if they did take it, we'd count it as a good thing, because it would be an indication that that employee wasn't the right fit after all."

"This is incredible," Max said. "It's not just about Callahan choosing its employees. It's about the employees choosing Callahan."

"That's a great way of putting it," Lisa agreed.

"This is the first time I've seen a company that talks about 'culture' and really puts it into action," Max said. "Of course it's a community if everyone is consciously choosing to be here. And it sounds like that choice is continual: With open, clear communication, you guys make sure that everyone—on *both* sides of the paycheck—is getting what they need."

Lisa nodded, pleased. "That's exactly my point. *That's* why I wanted you to come to HR today."

• • •

CORE VALUE #7

Communicate Clearly and Openly.

The key to effective communication is in both clear speaking and active listening. Consistent communication keeps us on the same page and moving in the same direction.

Chapter Eight

CORE VALUE #8

Recognize Individual and Company Success

Real leadership is leaders recognizing that they serve the people that they lead.
—Pete Hoekstra

"Dad, your tie is crooked."

Max was rushing out the door when his daughter's voice stopped him in his tracks. He turned around and bent down to her eight-year-old height.

"Will you fix it for me?" he asked, lifting his chin.

Wearing a very serious expression, she gave the tie a few tugs. "There," she said, sounding very businesslike. "That's much better."

Max straightened up and looked ruefully at his wife, Joanna, who had just let the babysitter in and was waiting for him by the front door. "I guess I've gotten out of practice tying my ties since I started at Callahan," he said. "Maybe I'm not a tie-wearing businessman-type anymore."

"I'm not sure I mind the change," Joanna said, reaching for his hand. "But you sure cleaned up nice tonight."

They were on their way to the Callahan Academy Awards. The employees had told Max this was the night to dress "like a rock star," so after much back-and-forth, he'd finally settled on a skinny black tie, a fedora, and dark sunglasses. Next to him, Joanna was striking in a midnight-purple cocktail dress—with a hot pink feather boa and her own pair of hot pink sunglasses.

For the last several days, as he steered his little desk around the company, Max had been getting more and more excited about this important evening. Ever since he had arrived at Callahan, he'd been hearing about the Callahan Academy Awards, a yearly celebration the company held for employees. But it was more than just your run-of-the-mill annual company party; it was also, as the name implied, an awards ceremony.

After hearing about the Doug Thompson Impactful Change Award from Arthur in the Packaging Department, Max couldn't wait to give one out. It struck him as the perfect motivator for the kind of values that made a difference not just for a company but for the people who worked there. He had decided he would continue to call it the Doug Thompson Award in honor of his predecessor, from whom he'd learned so much—even though he hadn't actually spoken with him in months.

The Doug Thompson Award was only one of many. All the Callahan employees had voted on nominees in categories that ranged from Best Attitude to Best Dressed, and yesterday they'd all gotten to vote for the winners in each category by secret ballot. A group of talented employees had been working on writing, producing, and editing video of the nominees at work, which would be shown during the awards ceremony. The whole evening would be not just a party, but a carefully designed event.

Max was looking forward to something he'd started to get used to around Callahan: spending time with people he genuinely liked and laughing. And he was also looking forward to finally introducing everyone to Joanna—and introducing her to the company he couldn't stop raving about. They gave their kids final goodbye kisses and reminded the babysitter that 9:30 was definitely bedtime, no matter what certain young people might think of it, and they headed out the door.

"You know, I think it's really cool that Callahan has this awards ceremony," Joanna said as Max pulled the car out of the driveway. "I mean, it's always great for a company to get together and have a nice evening to celebrate the employees, but I've never heard of doing it as an actual awards ceremony."

"Yeah," Max said. "I really agree. When Rhonda first told me about it, I kind of had my doubts—"

"And she won you over, just like she always does?" Joanna joked.

Max had to pause and think. Sure enough, he couldn't think of a single time that he'd heard about an unusual Callahan practice without ultimately deciding it made a lot of sense and he wanted to keep it in place.

"Well, the thing I was worried about," he explained, "is that, when they said awards, they meant it would be one of those things where the top salesperson gets a bonus or something. And the CEO decides every award and who's worthy and who's coming up short. And I thought—should we really be doing that? Doesn't that just stoke competition and getting cutthroat with the people who should be on your side? But as it turns out, that's not it at all. You should have seen how much all of the employees were participating in getting this ready over the last week or so. They're scrambling for the opportunity to reward each other."

"And they're really in charge of recognizing each other, right?" Joanna asked.

"Exactly. They nominate each other. They vote on the winner. I'm only giving one award."

"It seems like it's a really supportive place to work."

"It is," Max said thoughtfully. "Kind of a change for me."

Joanna smiled. "I think you're finally finding the right fit for you," she said.

Max nodded. "I couldn't have guessed it when Doug first called me, but I think you're right. I think Callahan is the kind of company I've been looking for all this time.

"And you know what's interesting about it?" Max continued. "I think that was true for a lot of the employees at Callahan. It's like a magnet that sort of draws in the right kind of people. And once the right people are there, Callahan treats them well so they stay there. Do you know what I just found out? We've got this great kid working on the Packaging Department floor, Dean Trumbell. A really motivated young man. You remember I told you we're going to bring him along on the trip to El Salvador in a few months?"

"Oh yeah," Joanna said. "I do remember you mentioned him. Sounds like he's really motivated and deserves to move up."

"Exactly!" Max said. "And at Callahan, it turns out that kind of thing is actually *possible*. I was bragging about Dean to our Director of Coffee, and he said, 'You know I worked my way up from the Packaging Department, right?' I was dumbfounded. He started there part-time when he was in high school, literally sweeping floors. I mean, the guy is really good. I assumed he had a thousand chemistry degrees and a résumé the length of a football field—but he's been with Callahan his whole career!"

"Wow," Joanna said, genuinely impressed.

"And that's not the only example, either. Remember our Director of Sales and Marketing, Jasmine?"

"Yup," said Joanna. From Max's stories, she already felt like she knew most of the Callahan employees herself.

"She started out as a regular salesperson. And now she's heading up two departments. And she's intimidatingly good at it. She might just help me save the company with that Waterbury deal."

Joanna nodded, remembering the important potential customer, a chain of East Coast coffeehouses that

Max had been courting for weeks and that could very well put an end to Callahan's financial woes.

"It seems like good policy," she said, referring back to Jasmine. "If people are doing well within the company, and they already know the ethos and the business, why not reward them for their hard work? Why go outside the company and have to start at zero every time?"

"Right," Max agreed. "It's not just good people policy, it's good business sense. It makes so much sense that they put it in writing in their Core Values."

"Oh, I know this one!" Joanna interrupted. "It's Core Value number eight ...

Recognize Individual and Company Success.

Right? Did I guess it right?"

Max nearly steered the car into a ditch. "How did you know that?"

Joanna shrugged mischievously. "You keep talking about how smart the Core Values are, so I stole a copy off your desk at home. I'm trying to think of sly ways to slip them in under the radar with the other managers at work." Joanna was a manager at a PR firm downtown— and had often commented on the ironic discrepancy between the firm's area of business and its attitude toward people.

"I gotta say," Max laughed, "it wouldn't hurt to try."

They had arrived at Callahan ... which was wholly transformed. A red carpet led them to the front door, through a crowd of Callahan employees all decked out in flashy—even outlandish—outfits. Max and Joanna weren't the only ones in sunglasses even though it was well past sunset.

Just inside the front entrance, a photographer was taking pictures of employees posing in front of a wall-sized Callahan logo. Further inside, the desks on the sales floor had been cleared out to make room for banquet tables draped in white linen. At the front of the room was a podium and a huge screen for projections. All the Callahan employees were milling about carrying drinks with brightly colored paper umbrellas. A DJ was playing music, and some of the employees had already started a spur-of-the-moment dance contest.

The evening was a blur as Max took Joanna around the room, with hardly a moment between employees rushing up and exclaiming, "This must be Joanna!" Everyone was thrilled to meet her, and Max was just as thrilled to share Callahan with her.

But what he was really waiting for were the awards. A hush fell over the crowd as the employees took their seats and the room dimmed for the videos. Different employees had been specially selected to present each award, and as each of them stood up, they got everyone laughing or remembering a moment from the previous year fondly. The video projections—which had at first made budget-conscious Max feel a little doubtful—were the best part. Just like the clips from Oscar-nominated films that roll before each award is presented, the videos showed employees in hilarious or triumphant moments as swelling music played in the background.

And then it was Max's turn to present the Doug Thompson Impactful Change Award. He gave Joanna's hand a squeeze and went up to the podium.

"You know, it's funny," he told the crowd of employees—and new friends—at Callahan. "The person whom I've selected to win this award this year was actually the first one to talk to me about how important it is to Callahan that we constantly embrace change. But when I went back and looked in Doug's records, I found that this particular employee hadn't yet been selected for the award. He's not in it for the award. He's in it because he's genuinely curious about what's the best way, the next development, how to improve.

" 'Is this still the best way of doing things?' He's always asking that question. Just like, as I gather, Doug Thompson was always asking that question. And just like I've learned—from the winner of this award and from all of you—to keep asking that question. So without further ado, ladies and gentlemen, I present to you the winner of this year's Doug Thompson Impactful Change Award ... Arthur Brooks!"

The whole room was on its feet in an instant as Arthur made his way up to the podium. Arthur's broad shoulders were practically bursting the seams of his suit, and the moment he got up to the podium, he enveloped Max in a massive bear hug. Max clapped him on the back and handed him his small trophy emblazoned with the Callahan logo. Max had never been prouder to recognize the work of an employee who deserved it.

• • •

CORE VALUE #8

Recognize Individual and Company Success.

Callahan is not a place that fosters feelings of jealousy or envy. We will root for and celebrate each other's accomplishments and be there for each other during disappointments. Love is the attitude we will demonstrate with everyone we are in contact with.

CHAPTER NINE

CORE VALUE #9

Protect Our Commitment to Quality

Quality is never an accident; it is always the result of high intention, sincere effort, intelligent direction, and skillful execution; it represents the wise choice of many alternatives.
—William A. Foster

THE NEXT week found Max in the Roasting Department. After telling Joanna about the background of Callahan's Director of Coffee, Carter Simmons, Max started to think that Roasting was the obvious next stop for his rolling desk. After all, he was CEO of Callahan Coffee Roasters. Shouldn't he start getting an in-depth understanding of the roasting process?

Max and Carter were already very familiar with each other—Director of Coffee was one of the company's upper-level positions, so Carter had been working closely with Max and Randall, the CFO, on the business plan that would extricate Callahan from its tight financial spot. They had come up with a plan for proceeding without replacing the revenue lost when their major customer moved on, but their preferred plan would of course be to simply replace that revenue with a new revenue stream from Waterbury Coffeehouses, the East Coast chain.

At this point, they had done everything possible to secure Waterbury's business, from demonstrating Callahan's creativity and unique approach with that *Goldilocks* book to putting together a proposal that would not only provide Waterbury with outstanding coffee but also offer them substantial savings over Callahan's primary East Coast competitor—even after the greater shipping distances were factored in. And as hard as Max was working to secure the Waterbury deal, he was working just as hard on his project of getting to know Callahan from the inside, wheeling his rolling desk from department to department.

Carter met Max just inside the door of the large warehouse room where the roasting took place. Carter was an energetic man in his late thirties. He had, as Max knew, been with Callahan from the beginning, and if anyone knew coffee—it was him. In fact, the system he had developed early on for training roast masters, from their apprenticeships through journeymen standing to advanced positions, had been adopted as the industry standard. The governing body that certified roasters in the U.S., the American Specialty Coffee Alliance, now used Carter's criteria for qualifying roast masters as the nationwide standard.

Carter extended a welcoming hand as Max came wheeling his desk into the Roasting Department. "So, Max, what are you hoping to learn today? Why did you pick the Roasting Department for your next stop?"

"Well," Max said, "this strikes me as the first and most important place for me to get to know Core Value number nine ...

Protect Our Commitment to Quality.

I'm here to get an eyewitness understanding of why our coffee is so renowned for quality."

Carter grinned. "You've come to the right place. I mean, honestly, anywhere in Callahan would have been the right place when it comes to high quality, but we might as well start with the quality of our coffee since coffee is the main reason we're here. As far as our coffee goes, we don't think of quality as a destination, but something that we're constantly watching, analyzing, and improving. You know we won Roaster of the Year from *Coffee Roasters Monthly*, right?"

How could Max forget? The framed award was hanging on the wall of his new office, which was still waiting for him to move in. *Coffee Roasters Monthly* was a major industry magazine, with distribution throughout the country, so the distinction meant a great deal to Callahan.

"But did you know we got runner-up for four years in a row before we won the fifth year—last year?" Carter asked.

"Actually, no, nobody mentioned that!" Max said.

"Yup. And believe me, runner-up amongst that field of competitors would have been a fine place to just hang out and coast. But not to us. We keep pursuing excellence. And the recognition we finally got isn't just for the quality of our coffee; they also factor in our sustainability practices and our business practices, especially how we treat our people."

"Then frankly, it doesn't surprise me that we won," Max said.

"We worked hard for it. I know you're a football fan—there's a Vince Lombardi quote that I really like:

'The quality of a person's life is in direct proportion to their commitment to excellence, regardless of their chosen field of endeavor.' That's exactly how we work at Callahan. Of course we're constantly striving to make our coffee excellent; that's the foundation. But that commitment goes through the whole organization, from our sales reps to our customer service, from the billing and collections process through to delivery."

"I have to agree," Max said. "And I've got the view from my rolling desk to prove it! In fact, I told Waterbury that we cultivate a culture of quality."

"Perfect way of putting it," Carter said. The two of them had wandered over to one of the roasting machines, where freshly roasted coffee beans were spinning in a large, round cooling tray. "Actually, here's an example. This coffee is an extremely high-end variety. We include it in a blend of six coffees that gives folks a layered flavor. This is the most expensive variety in the blend, so we could lower the percentage of it and up the percentage of a cheaper coffee by 5 percent or so. Most people wouldn't taste the difference. But we would know. We formulated the blend very carefully; we found exactly the right combination. So, if we tweaked it, we'd know we had compromised the quality. We just wouldn't do that."

"I definitely approve of that," Max said.

"And that commitment doesn't stop just because we've found a particular coffee or created a particular blend we like," Carter said. "We taste every single batch of coffee that comes out of here, which is literally dozens and dozens per day. If it's not up to our standards, we start over."

"I would expect nothing less," Max replied, feeling genuinely proud to hear his Director of Coffee standing up for his standards before he had to say anything himself. "And this is why I'm not worried about Callahan." He glanced around and lowered his voice a touch. "Listen, I know I came here with a reputation. People knew of me as the takeover guy who guts companies to save them from the brink. I know people were afraid I'd be laying folks off.

"I just want you to know that that might have been my business-school-approved strategy and that it worked for me at other kinds of companies. But Callahan has completely transformed my philosophy. Everyone here is essential because everyone plays a specific and vital role in maintaining the kind of quality you're talking about. And it's that kind of quality that makes Callahan strong.

"Even if we don't seal the deal with Waterbury—which I have every confidence we will—Jasmine and I have already researched a number of similar-sized chains to approach. We're going to beat this thing with the best weapons we've got: our quality and our people."

Carter didn't even need to voice his agreement. It was clear from the expression on his face that he believed Max 100 percent.

● ● ●

CORE VALUE #9

Protect Our Commitment to Quality.

Quality is inherent in everything we do. Our quality is not just reflected in our outstanding coffee but also in our attention to detail, our innovations, and our service. Our commitment to delivering quality in all interactions must be protected through our daily decisions and strategies for the future.

CHAPTER TEN

CORE VALUE #10

Be Friendly and Have a Sense of Humor

*You can make more friends in two months by
becoming interested in other people than you
can in two years by trying to get other people
interested in you.*
—Dale Carnegie

IT WAS nine in the morning. Max was ready for another day of work ... but his little rolling desk was nowhere to be found. He usually parked it in his office overnight and then picked it up each morning and either wheeled at random or headed off to a department he hadn't yet visited.

This morning he planned to check out the Finance Department; he was particularly interested in sitting down with Brenda Daniels, who handled purchasing, to ask her how she went about selecting vendors and keeping costs down—without compromising quality or shared values.

But where was his desk? Max was sure he had left it against the wall by his office door. That was its spot. And where else would he put it? It's not like a person could easily misplace a desk on wheels.

Feeling a little lost and foolish, Max cast around and finally found a clipboard. It wasn't the same as a desk surface, but it would have to do for now. He had checked ahead with Brenda and promised to meet her first thing in the morning, and he didn't want to keep her waiting. Off to the Finance Department he would go, desk or no desk.

As he rounded the corner to the open office space where the Finance Department employees worked, he nearly ran smack into a tiny little Callahan Coffee Roasters truck.

"Surprise!" A collective shout came up from the Finance employees, who were standing in a big clump around the truck.

Max looked closer. It was his desk.

It had been decked out with poster board on all sides to look like a little truck, complete with cab and trailer. Someone—Max was guessing the Finance folks had enlisted the help of the Design Department—had intricately crafted the whole thing to look just like one of the Callahan delivery trucks, from the company logo on the side down to a very detailed and convincing miniature front grille.

"Ladies and gentlemen," announced Brenda, who was standing at the front of the group of Finance employees, "a belated Callahan Academy Award for Best Driver goes to Max Anderson!"

Everyone applauded and cheered. Max laughed.

"When on earth did you guys do this?" he asked, admiring his new little truck/desk. It was, for better or worse, not lost on him that for the rest of his rolling desk project, he would have to accept looking very much like a toddler driving a Big Wheel around the company.

Brenda smiled. "The idea started in the Finance Department, but everybody on staff was in on it. Ted stole the desk out of your office after you left on Friday. And some of the guys from the Design Department had the panels ready to go—they just had to come in a little early to attach them."

"I'm very honored to accept this award," Max said, in a jokingly solemn tone. "I will drive this desk with pride."

The Finance Department employees began to return to their desks as Brenda said to Max, "Glad you like it. It's our way of bringing home Core Value number ten ...

Be Friendly and Have a Sense of Humor.

We figured by now you've lived enough of our Core Values to take it in stride if we make your desk look a little goofier than it already did."

"Wait a minute," Max said, pretending to be shocked. "My desk looked goofy before?"

"To be honest," Brenda said, laughing, "it's starting to get a reputation around here. I think people are going to miss it when you finally move into your office."

"You know, I am too," Max said. "But for now, I'm still on the road! And as long as I'm driving around learning from people, maybe you can clear up this question I've had ever since I first read the Core Values. How do you get people to 'be friendly and have a sense of humor'? I mean, is that really something you can mandate?"

"Yes and no," Brenda said. "First, Callahan chooses a special kind of employee who shares our values. I'm sure Lisa in HR showed you how our twenty-two questions during the hiring process go a long way toward showing us a person's creative, humorous side."

"Sure," Max agreed.

"But mostly, 'Have fun' is in our mission statement because it's so important. We don't necessarily mean just having fun at work—we mean making work fun. Because if we're having fun, then we're team building and we're stoking passion for what we sell."

"I see," Max said. "I don't see anyone slacking off and playing Ping Pong just for the sake of having fun, but I do often feel like I had a really fun day at Callahan—without even trying."

"That's exactly what I mean," Brenda said. "Asking people to have a sense of humor isn't just so we have an office full of comedians. It's about having a lighthearted atmosphere so we can meet challenges without getting overwhelmed. It's about not taking things personally, but instead going along with what the team decides is best for the company. And, sure, every now and then it's about playing jokes on your friends."

Max laughed. "I did hear somebody say the other day that instead of *Help people, make friends, have fun*, our mission statement should be 'Help people make fun of their friends.' "

Brenda grinned. "Yup. That's about right. Especially here in the *Fun*-ance Department."

Max groaned. "Nothing says 'fun' like a good pun,"

he said, figuring if Brenda could dress his serious CEO's desk up like a child's toy, he could skewer her punning.

"But seriously," Brenda said, "there's something really important behind this Core Value that goes beyond making sure employees are happy and having a good time—as important as that is. What's really serious about being friendly is that it's organization-wide, and it's not about exclusivity."

"How do you mean?" Max asked.

"Well, we're friendly amongst ourselves, and we don't create cliques. Anybody can come have fun in the Fun-ance Department. But we go even further than that. We treat our vendors with the same friendliness and open-ness as our fellow employees. And our competitors too."

"Really?"

"Absolutely. You'll never hear us compare ourselves to the competition by putting them down. And we allow any competitors who are interested to take a full tour."

Now this was new to Max, who was used to having a team of lawyers demand nondisclosure agreements before the tiniest meetings. "You're not worried about trade secrets?"

Brenda shrugged. "No. I mean, we don't open up our financial records and spread them around the room. But if competitors want to see our roasting process or taste coffee with us, they can."

"And it's never been a problem?"

"Never," Brenda said, shaking her head. "In fact, we actually had the opposite problem—somebody tried to share a competitor's secrets with us."

"What happened?" Max asked.

"We had a guy call us and say he wanted to meet with us about a possible job as a salesperson. When he came in, it turned out that he had worked for a competitor, and he brought their customer list along with him. It had everything there—phone numbers, how much they purchased and when ... everything. And instead of hiring that guy and taking the list, we called the competitor and let them know what had happened."

"Good for you!" Max said, impressed.

"We treat others the way we want to be treated," Brenda said. "And that includes holding others to the same standards we hold ourselves to."

"Sounds like a value I can get on board with," Max said.

Brenda raised an eyebrow, grinning. "You're already on board," she said, and rapped her knuckles on the top of Max's desk—which was now the roof of his truck.

• • •

CORE VALUE #10

Be Friendly and Have a Sense of Humor.

When you walk through our front door, you will most likely hear two things: one is the sound of fresh espresso being ground, the other is the echo of true laughter. We work hard but have a great time doing it. We never take ourselves too seriously and believe that laughter is the best medicine.

CHAPTER ELEVEN

CORE VALUE #11
Serve Our Community and Each Other

So long as we love we serve. So long as we are loved by others, I would almost say that we are indispensible, and no man is useless while he has a friend.
—Robert Louis Stevenson

MAX HATED to admit it, but it was almost time to park his desk (or ... his tiny truck) and settle into his office. He had visited all of the Callahan departments. He knew every last employee by name. And when the Monday Morning Meetings rolled around, he could recite each and every core value without even looking at the poster on the wall.

He no longer thought of himself as the "turnaround guy," hired to save Callahan from doom and destruction. He simply thought of himself as the CEO of a successful company—a company that was actively working to rebuild its revenue, sure, but not a company that was in any way under threat. Max was almost ready to move into his office and continue at the helm of a robust, thriving organization.

But there was one last person he wanted to sit down with. Max was almost ashamed to remember that this person held a position that, in his early days at Callahan, he had planned to cut. But by now, he knew it was perhaps the most indispensible role in the whole company. The Director of Culture and Community Relations.

Max wheeled his desk up to Eric Gordon's office door. He didn't need to knock because the door was standing wide open—as usual. It could just as soon be taken off its hinges, and Eric probably wouldn't even notice.

Before the miniature front grille of the Callahan truck-desk had even appeared in the doorway, Eric had jumped up from his desk and come forward to greet Max with his usual warm handshake and broad smile. He was fairly young, but—like many others at Callahan—he had worked his way up in the company, and had actually been the one to suggest his position to Doug Thompson.

Over time, Callahan had started so many programs to support its community of employees and to help them reach out to the community outside the company that Eric came to Doug and said, "You know, I was thinking we'd benefit from managing all of these programs more centrally." Doug had agreed with Eric's pitch, and so for the last five years, Eric had been managing all of the programs that defined Callahan's approach to building and sustaining community.

Eric was a gregarious, curly-haired young man who had an almost uncanny knack for connecting with every person who crossed his path. When Max arrived, he had already prepared for their meeting by pulling up several different windows on his wide desktop monitor so that he could show Max exactly what he was working on.

Max pulled up a seat next to Eric. "All right," he said, "let's get right to it. I've been hearing about all the extraordinary ways that Callahan creates a feeling of community. And I have to be frank, when I first came here, I would have thought of those kinds of programs as unnecessary fluff. But after seeing the way people at Callahan work together, I'm starting to think it's the key to the whole company."

Eric nodded, clearly pleased with Max's one-eighty. "I tend to agree. I mean, we work together well because we care about each other. And I think of my position as supporting that company philosophy. The more we feel like a community, the better we are at making and selling coffee, the better we do as a business ... and the more we feel like a community. It's exactly what keeps us on track."

"I agree with that right from the outset. But tell me about the programs that support that community spirit," Max said. "How do you actually go about implementing something that seems so hard to define?"

"Let me give you my favorite example," Eric said. "The Callahan Family Relief Fund. It's a fund that our employees have the *option* to contribute to—but they're not required to in any way. They can opt to have between $1 and $100 come out of each paycheck automatically and go into the fund."

"And what do you use the fund for?"

"If anything unexpected happens to a Callahan employee, any kind of hardship, like a medical expense that insurance won't quite cover, the employee can apply to the fund for relief. We have a committee that reviews applications, and if they approve, they just grant that Callahan employee the money. It's a no-strings-attached grant. It never has to be paid back."

"That's a phenomenal idea," Max said, enthused. "So who sits on the committee?"

"It changes all the time," Eric answered, "because the fund belongs to all of us. Doug and I were permanent members, and then any other employees can volunteer to join us and they rotate out after a year." Eric turned to Max and looked him squarely in the eye. "We were a bit worried in the beginning that this was the kind of program that might get cut because of the extra time and expense it takes to administer. So I've been waiting to ask you until you got more settled in if this was something you'd want to participate in."

"Are you kidding?" Max asked. "Count me in!"

Eric grinned. "I thought you'd say that. I'm glad."

"But I have more questions about it," Max said. "What's an example of something you've used it for recently?"

"I've got one ready for you," Eric said, pointing to his computer screen. "This is an application we approved just a few weeks ago."

Max recognized the name of the employee at the top of the application right away. "Oh yeah—Cristina's father passed away; I remember she took a few weeks off to go be with her family in Spain."

"Right," Eric said. "But since it was a last-minute flight, it was well over a thousand dollars for her airplane ticket. So we paid for it."

"That's great," Max said. "I'm so glad she had that

recourse. How much would you say you grant out each year?"

"Last year we gave about eleven thousand," he said.

"Not bad," Max said. "But you said it's optional for employees to contribute? Do you always have enough?"

"That's the really cool thing about it. We don't have a single employee who doesn't contribute to the fund in some way, large or small."

Max smiled. "I should have guessed."

"Yup. It's all about Core Value number eleven ...

Serve Our Community and Each Other.

But the thing that I think is really great about this value," Eric continued, "is that when we really foster the attitude of taking care of Callahan community, we find that people feel encouraged to help others way beyond Callahan. And we've got programs that support that, too."

"Like the Global Children's Fund?" Max asked.

"Exactly!"

This was another program that Max had been a little bewildered by when he first came on board but that he'd gone along with because he certainly couldn't argue with the sentiment behind it. A few days after he first arrived at Callahan, Rhonda had brought him a folder with the photo and the name of a little girl in Colombia. As Rhonda explained, Callahan sponsored a child in a coffee-growing country on behalf of every single employee. The employees could write letters back and forth with the children and contribute extra money if they wanted to. After a few weeks, Max actually had gotten pretty absorbed in the letter-writing, and his kids had gotten on board too, excited to have a pen pal in another country.

"We've had that program in place from the very beginning," Eric explained. "Doug started it when he first founded Callahan. And since then, we've donated over $250,000 to children around the world."

"I love it," Max said. "But I see you've got a bunch more windows open on your computer. Tell me about some other programs."

Eric clicked over to another window. "Well, we're all about using the product we create to be useful to others. So here is a list of the nonprofit organizations that are able to buy coffee from us at steep discounts." He clicked to another screen. "And this is about our partnership with local food banks and shelters. We donate coffee to them, of course, but we also require that employees volunteer at the food bank on occasion. It's considered part of their job."

"And there's also the special coffee you sell around the holidays, right? I think Carter mentioned something about that."

"Oh yeah!" Eric said. "I'm glad you asked. We have a special blend of coffee that we sell in specially marked packaging before the holidays. And one dollar from each bag we sell goes to Toys for Tots. But we've also got our own holiday program right around here."

"How so?" Max asked.

"Well, when the holidays roll around, you'll see two trees in the lobby where employees can drop off presents. One of the trees is for the community, and one of them is just for employees. As you know, not every position here is high-level and high-paying, so we've got that 'giving tree' that's covered with envelopes. You pick an envelope off the tree, and it'll tell you, 'A nine-year-old child wants a train,' or something like that. You don't know which employee's kid it is or anything. But you can go ahead and get that child the train set."

Max had just started to say, "I can't wait to pick an envelope—" when suddenly a huge shout went up from the sales floor outside Eric's office. Max stood up so fast he banged his knee on his rolling desk. He was sure that something had gone wrong. Was someone hurt?

But then he realized that the shout was actually a cheer. A moment later, Jasmine rushed through the open door of Eric's office, followed by several other salespeople.

"We got it!" she cried.

"Got what?" Max almost shouted, swept up by the group's enthusiasm.

"The Waterbury deal!"

Again, as if hearing the news for the first time, the salespeople broke into cheers and applause. For a brief moment, Max was struck silent. And then he joined in the cheers.

"Everyone," Max said, when the cheering had died down, "I've been meaning to say this for a long time, and this is the perfect chance. I want to say that, quite frankly, I knew we'd get this deal. I knew it because of what I've seen of this company in the weeks since I first came here.

"I arrived thinking this was a company with financial problems that needed a personnel overhaul to get itself out of trouble. And what I discovered is that this is a company with a personnel solution to any financial problem. Callahan's people are rooted in its values, and the product is supported by that solid foundation. Without that formula, we'd be in real trouble. And that formula is exactly what got us out of trouble."

Max turned to Eric. "Programs like the ones Eric is running are the kind of thing I might have cut in my old life. And now I understand that programs like Callahan's are at the root of a successful company. You can't make and market and sell a good product without good people and good values. And that's why we got this deal. And that's why we'll continue to get and keep business."

Everyone applauded again, Jasmine loudest of all. Just then, Max's little rolling desk caught his eye.

"We've got a lot of people waiting to hear this news," Max said. "And I'm going to take one last spin around the company to tell them."

And with that, he wheeled his desk out into the halls of Callahan.

• • •

CORE VALUE #11

Serve Our Community and Each Other.

We believe that we are not obligated, but moved to donate time and resources to lift up each other and the people in our surrounding communities. We do so with an attitude of gratitude that we are fortunate enough to help.

BREW OUR AWARD WINNING COFFEES
FROM THE COMFORT OF YOUR OWN HOME

Sourcing coffees of authentic quality requires tireless dedication and strong international ties. These values are the foundation that Dillanos green coffee sourcing is built on. Roasting is a craft that requires skill, passion and a deep understanding of how the smallest time and temperature adjustments can affect the development of the coffee.

ORDER ONLINE:
DILLANOS.COM

OR CALL US TO ORDER:
1.800.234.5282 (9AM-5PM PACIFIC)

DILLANOS
COFFEE ROASTERS

CPSIA information can be obtained
at www.ICGtesting.com
Printed in the USA
FSOW04n0817070617
35074FS